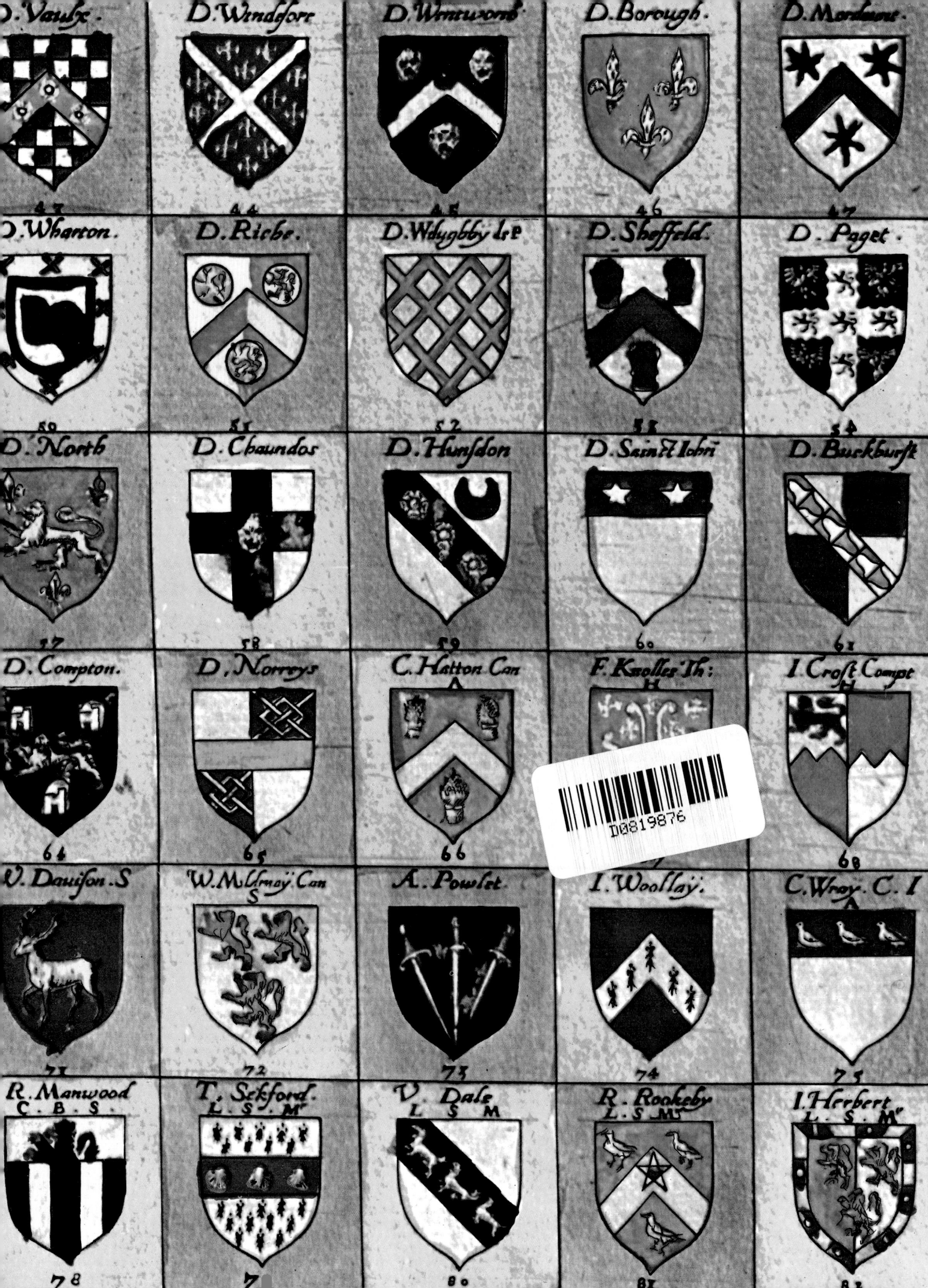

CURTIS INTERNATIONAL
PORTRAITS OF GREATNESS

•

General Editor
Enzo Orlandi

Text by
Massimo Rossaro

Translator
C. J. Richards

Published by
ARNOLDO MONDADORI EDITORE
and
THE CURTIS PUBLISHING COMPANY

THE
LIFE
&
TIMES
OF

ELIZABETH

CURTIS BOOKS
A division of
The Curtis Publishing Company
Philadelphia • New York

QUEEN MARY'S RING

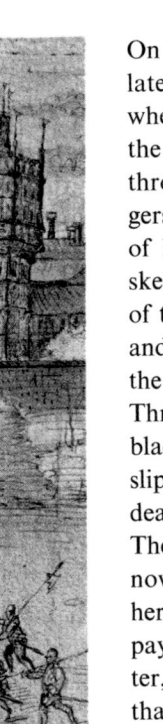

On the morning of November 17, 1558, a gray day in late autumn, heavy with mists lying over silent fields where agricultural labors had long since come to a stop, the winding road from London to Hatfield House was thronged with unaccustomed traffic. Groups of messengers on horseback made the air resound with the clatter of hooves, the wind from their gallop stripping the skeletal trees of their last leaves. Then came the Lords of the Council, wearing gold chains about their necks and black cloaks of mourning which reached almost to the ground. Following these cantered Sir Nicholas Throckmorton, a gentleman of the court carrying the black and gold engagement ring which he had just slipped off the finger of Mary Tudor, laid out on her death bed in her Palace in London.

The Queen had died at the first glimmer of dawn, and now these people who had awaited for days the end of her slow death had come to Elizabeth's residence to pay homage to the new Queen, Mary Tudor's half sister, once known as the "Little Bastard." For years— that is, since her miraculous escape from the axe—she had been living in ostentatious retirement, half chatelaine, half country woman, far from the Court. But silent, secretive, wary as only the persecuted can be, she had never lost sight of the Crown. She had learned to trust no one. To Throckmorton, who had been predicting her sister's death for some time, she had retorted that she would not believe it until she had seen the ring which never left Mary's hand. This was why he was galloping with the jewel tucked into his jerkin. But the Lords of the Council had preceded him. They found the new Queen walking on the lawn: a pale slender girl with dark eyes and flame-colored hair who, upon seeing them, had stopped under a large oak.

When she heard their news, she knelt on the cold grass amid the crackling autumn leaves, saying, "This is the Lord's doing; it is marvelous in our eyes," a quotation from the Psalms (118, v. 23) which celebrates God's mercy toward Israel. Elizabeth quoted the Bible, which pleased the Protestants; she quoted it in Latin, which pleased the Catholics. With these first words: uttered upon becoming Queen, her ambivalent attitude toward the warring religious factions became apparent.

The Chancellors Seat.

Below: King Henry VIII from a portrait of the school of Holbein. The mark of his pride and inflexibility is plain to see. This monarch, born in 1491, first had been destined for the Church. The early death of his elder brother Arthur left him heir to the English throne, which he occupied at the age of 18 in 1509.

Right: Two miniatures in the British Museum showing scenes in the life of Henry VIII. In the first the court jester, Will Somers, stands next to the king, apparently unable to amuse him. In the second the King is shown holding an open prayer book. Before the schism with Rome, Henry was noted for his piety and faith.

Opposite page: An allegorical painting showing Henry VIII with the children who reigned after him. To the King's left is his immediate successor, Edward VI. He is holding in his hand the red rose of the House of Lancaster from which the Tudors descended. Edward died in his adolescence, leaving his half-sister Mary, Henry's daughter by his first wife, to succeed him. She is on the other side of the throne with her consort, Philip of Spain. They are followed by the allegorical figure of War. On the other hand, Elizabeth, standing next to her brother, is accompanied by the allegorical figures that typified her reign—Peace and Plenty, the latter bearing symbolic fruit.

THE
NEW QUEEN

"Remember old King Harry the Eighth!" shouted an unidentified man of the people facing the crowd, while the young Queen moved forward to her coronation one frosty and gleaming winter morning. A storm of cheers answered him, for indeed the people of London had not forgotten the ribald and magnificent Henry VIII and eagerly sought a resemblance to him in the face of his daughter. Her flaming hair, her clear complexion, the imperious look in her eye were all his. Hers also his quick temper and ready laughter, as well as his sensitivity to the moods of the common people.

These Tudors—there never was a ruling family which could equal their popularity. Perhaps it was because they belonged entirely to their country. Except for Mary, with her mother's Spanish blood, the others were English, body and soul; their virtues and vices, although monstrously magnified by royalty and violence, were those of their subjects. For this reason, because they recognized themselves in their monarchs, the people accepted Tudor mistakes and excesses with no diminishing of their loyalty. Henry VIII had managed throughout his reign to preserve his popularity with the English people; the magic was repeated for Elizabeth. Henry had succeeded in imposing a new policy on his subjects, a new religion,

a separation from the Pope, a break with tradition—for the sole purpose of putting on the throne beside him the woman who had bewitched him, and from whom he had hoped for a son: Anne Boleyn. And because the Vatican refused to annul his marriage with the legitimate Queen, Catherine of Aragon, Henry declared himself Supreme Head of the Church of England, repudiated his first wife, and had his new one crowned. But the male heir never came from her; instead there had been a little girl, Elizabeth, she whom the people were now acclaiming on her way to Westminster. When the procession started from the Tower of London—prison as well as Royal Residence—perhaps her thoughts turned to the mother she had scarcely known who had been sleeping for more than 20 years, a headless skeleton, in the chapel of the Tower. Anne's fairy tale had not lasted long. When the enchantment had been dispelled, the King had accused her of adultery, saying he had been seduced with Black Magic. A jury of Peers of the Realm, among whom sat her own father, Thomas Boleyn, adjudged her guilty and condemned her to death: her head fell under the executioner's axe. And Elizabeth, daughter of that unhappy marriage, was proclaimed illegitimate.

FRAIL EDWARD AND BLOODY MARY

Left: Portrait of Mary Tudor by a painter of the Flemish School. Below: Painting by an unknown artist of the 16th century showing the boy king, Edward VI, with his advisers. His father on his death bed designated him as his successor; at his feet are the Pope, Catholic priests and monks who opposed him during his reign.

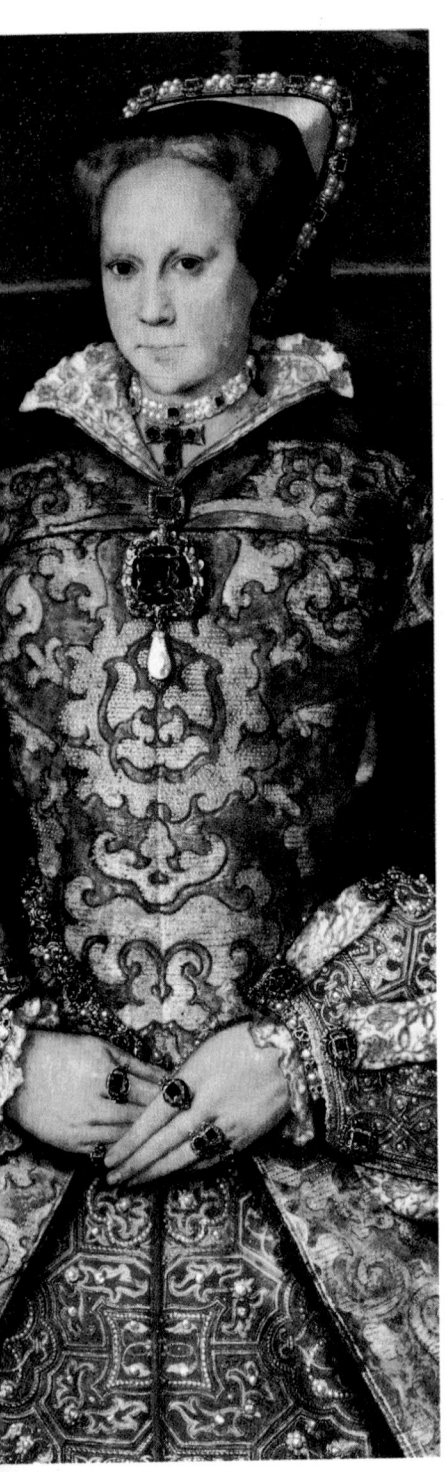

Having buried one wife and beheaded a second one, Henry had not lost faith in the institution of marriage. Indeed, as Anne was climbing the steps to the executioner's block, her replacement had already been found. A few days later he led this one to the altar. Her name was Jane Seymour, and she was beguilingly fair and blonde. She at last gave the King the son he had wanted so much, Edward, but his birth cost his mother her life, and the baby grew into frail childhood. None of Henry's three subsequent marriages produced any progeny, and all of them ended badly: one in divorce, another on the executioner's block, and the last with Henry's death at 56.

All three of Henry's children were destined to reign, and their respective reigns became the rallying point of the opposing religious and political factions which were agitating England at that time. Edward was the first, a frail 10-year-old, maneuvered by a gang of ambitious and unscrupulous lords. In the fifth year of his reign the Protestants gained the upper hand. And the bland religious reforms instituted by Henry VIII which, apart from challenging the supremacy of the Pope, had not been intended to move very far from Catholic practices, were soon used as a weapon of persecution against the Catholics. On the death of the young king, at 16, the crown passed to his half-sister, Mary, daughter of Henry and Catherine of Aragon. Mary was to go down in history as "Catholic Mary" to the Catholics and "Bloody Mary" to the Protestants. Actually, Mary was the exact replica of her brother, with the difference that while intolerance under his reign was directed against the Church of Rome, her intolerance was directed against the Reformation. In this war Catholic excesses succeeded Protestant ones. For the third time in less than 20 years England changed religions. The Prince Consort, Philip of Spain, naturally gave his support to Mary. Thus the English masses, who had already largely been won over to the Reformation, coupled in their dislike the Catholics and the Spaniards. Blood soon flowed; people were burned at the stake on the sinister plain of Smithfield, at the gates of the capital. More than 300 people died in this horrible way during the last years of Mary's reign. And the people of London, thinking of the silent girl living in seclusion in the country, murmured among themselves: "God save our Elizabeth!"

THE ENDVR
WORDE ETH
OF THE FOR
LORD EVER

CVPERSTICION

OLATRY

ALL FLESHE
IS GRASSE

A COUNTRY ON THE BRINK OF RUIN

As she ascended the throne, Elizabeth found a country on the verge of ruin, devastated by the plague, torn by religious dissension and involved in a catastrophic war against France. The treasury coffers were empty, the result of the mad extravagances of her father and of the disastrous financial policies of Edward and Mary. Elizabeth inherited some of the traits of this calculating and parsimonious forebear who kept his own account books. From the very beginning of her reign she inaugurated a program of tight economies. Her most pressing concern was to make peace with France after the disastrous war which cost her sister the last English foothold on the continent: Calais. Elizabeth hated war because it was costly and because she was a woman of sense and sensibility who recoiled from violence. Although she was sometimes forced to wage war, she always first tried diplomacy. She was parsimonious alike about English lives and about English money and her people were always grateful to her for this who had been forced gradually to devalue a currency that had been so strong in the days of Henry VII, the founder of the House of Tudor.

Above: A small gallery of characters in the Tudor period. From left to right: Henry VIII from a portrait by an unknown artist. Anne Boleyn or Bullen. An opera about her was written by Donizetti entitled "Anna Bolena." Edward, only son of Henry VIII and of his third wife, Jane Seymour, who died of childbed fever a few days after his birth. Catherine Parr, Henry's last wife. Widowed twice before, she married the King in 1543 and remained by his side until his death in January of 1547. Catherine Parr was the only one of Henry's wives who tried to give the royal children a taste of family life. They found it fairly peaceful after the stormy existence Henry had led during his previous marriages. Opposite page: Portrait of

Elizabeth aged about 13. Her resemblance to her brother Edward VI and her air of precocious gravity are striking. Elizabeth's youth had been an unhappy one, especially after the death of the 16-year-old King when his elder half-sister, Mary, succeeded him on the throne. During the latter's reign Elizabeth was the object of a constant surveillance which was not relaxed even when the Princess, on whom were centered the hopes of the Protestant Party, asked to be instructed in the Roman Catholic faith. During Wyatt's rebellion, whose objective was to put her on the throne, she was shut up in the Tower of London. She owed her survival only to the constancy with which she denied all participation in the plot.

REMNANTS OF THE MIDDLE AGES AND REFINEMENTS OF THE RENAISSANCE

In 16th-century English life there was a mixture of medieval crudeness and Renaissance refinement. Meals were Gargantuan. In an age when a large part of mankind was either dying of hunger or overeating, a 10-course meal seemed hardly sufficient for monks who had taken vows of abstinence. Among the privileged classes, eating became something of a rite. At 11 A.M. and 5 P.M., diners would gather around long oaken tables covered with damask. Place and precedence were a matter of rigid rule. Music was often played during the meal. The menus were not varied. Dinner offered beef, lamb, goat, pork, poultry, game, and every conceivable kind of fish, followed by elaborate desserts: jellies and sweetmeats in which the cooks outdid themselves in molding ships, coats-of-arms and heraldic beasts. Entertainment ran the gamut from plays to ballets, to masked balls, to games. Among these the favorites were bullbaiting and bearbaiting, a sport in which ferocious dogs were set against bears and bulls; the dogs wore no protection against the wild beasts. The public often returned from these spectacles spattered with blood but always in high spirits.

Opposite page: Painting by an unknown artist of the 16th century of a wedding feast held in the residence of Sir Henry Unton. Note the orchestra and boy actors. Above: A manufacturer of precision instruments around 1576. Above right: Contemporary wood engraving showing the interior of a bookshop of the same period. Below: More scenes in the daily life of Elizabethan times. Directly below: A private smoking room. Smoking was violently criticized by Elizabeth's successor, King James I. Far left: Diners entertained by musicians. Center: The laboratory of a distiller with the instruments of his trade. Right: An alchemist.

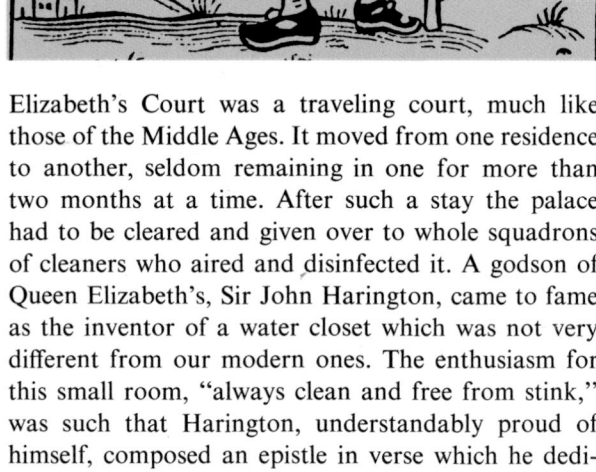

*Right: 16th-century wood engraving of an itinerant vendor.
Below: Typical bedroom of a nobleman in Elizabethan times. This one shows Sir Henry Unton attended by his physicians.
Bottom of page, left: Village feast with villagers dancing around a cart.
Right: Fishing, a pastime much favored in 16th-century England.*

Opposite page: Gallery in Knole Castle in Kent as it appeared during the reign of Queen Elizabeth. Note the enormous fireplace and the ceiling covered with geometric designs. Below: Two scenes of country life. England under Tudor reign was an almost totally agricultural country. The principal resources were farming and animal husbandry.

Elizabeth's Court was a traveling court, much like those of the Middle Ages. It moved from one residence to another, seldom remaining in one for more than two months at a time. After such a stay the palace had to be cleared and given over to whole squadrons of cleaners who aired and disinfected it. A godson of Queen Elizabeth's, Sir John Harington, came to fame as the inventor of a water closet which was not very different from our modern ones. The enthusiasm for this small room, "always clean and free from stink," was such that Harington, understandably proud of himself, composed an epistle in verse which he dedicated to the ladies-in-waiting on "their perfumed privy at Richmond."

In the summer, the entire Court set forth on long and festive visits to the country houses of illustrious families. These visits gave relief to the royal coffers, because all expenses had to be borne by each host in turn. Because of the honor and privilege which he derived from the visit, the host overlooked the financial drain it entailed. At the arrival of the Queen, people dressed in costumes as mythological characters would emerge from shrubberies and grottos to bow to the illustrious guest. But above all the passage of the royal Court was a memorable event which strengthened the bonds between Elizabeth and her people.

A WOMAN POSSESSED BY 100,000 DEVILS

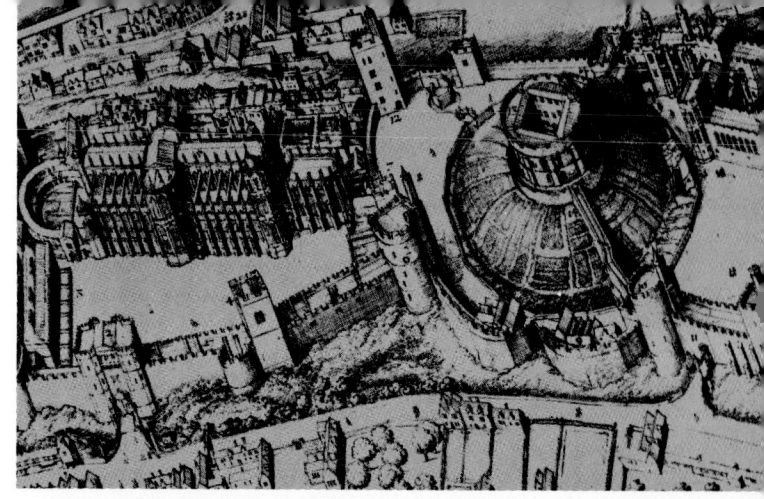

"My fondest wish," Elizabeth confided one day, when she was 26, to the Spanish ambassador, Bishop De Quadra, "would be to become a nun and to pass my days in a cell praying." Reporting back to his predecessor, Feria, the bishop commented: "Your Lordship will see what a pretty business it is to have to deal with this woman who I think must have 100,000 devils in her body, notwithstanding that she is forever repeating this sort of thing." Actually, the Catholics had not a clue as to what to expect from this Queen; furthermore, neither did the Protestants.

Her ascent to the throne was a relief to the followers of the Reformed Church, who had been forced during the reign of Queen Mary to perform the rites of the Roman Church if they did not wish to be burned at the stake. But if they had hoped to get back their own religion they had miscalculated. Elizabeth abhorred intolerance—a difficult attitude to understand in an age ruled by intolerance. During the reign of her half sister, she too had been obliged to forsake the Anglican faith in which she had been brought up and to ask to be instructed in the Roman faith. At the time of her ascent to the throne she knew quite well that the Protestants, who were in the majority in the capital, were in the minority in the provinces except in Kent and in Middlesex. Therefore she acted with great caution, a caution dictated not so much by political tact as by a sincere desire to reestablish peace in the realm.

The Coronation was performed according to Catholic rite; Archbishop Heath of York refused to officiate, but the Bishop of Carlisle was willing to substitute for him. Many people noticed the new Queen's efforts to seek compromise. Her ministers, headed by William Cecil—he too had learned during the days of Mary Tudor to follow a double standard—were pressing her to enforce her father's decrees upholding the Sovereign as Supreme Head of the Church. They wanted her to impose upon all parishes the use of the Book of Common Prayer and the reading of the service in English; nonetheless she remained opposed to all excesses and only asked of the Catholics the appearance of submission. In many castles priests living in hiding celebrated the Mass in Latin for the faithful in the neighborhood. Everyone was required to be present at the Anglican service, but the penalty for absence was not the stake, only a fine of twelvepence.

After the gloomy 12-year interval of the disastrous reigns of Edward VI and Mary Tudor, there reappeared at Elizabeth's Court the worldly splendor, the pursuit of pleasure and the refinement of culture which had already characterized her father's reign. She realized that one part of his popularity (so great that it survived a notable number of abuses of authority and of scandalous con-

Left: Windsor Castle, one of the favorite residences of Elizabeth's Court. Built on a promontory overlooking the Thames, it was rebuilt in 1344 by Edward III, who chose it as the meeting place of the Knights of the Garter which he had created. It had been enlarged and embellished by Henry VIII. Below: Anonymous contemporary painting, in the collection of Viscount de l'Isle, of a ball at the English court. The two dancers in the center are supposed to be the Queen and the Earl of Leicester. Passionately fond of music and poetry, Elizabeth was also a woman of great learning. She spoke French and Italian fluently. She translated Sallust and Boethius from the Latin and once rebuked the Polish ambassador in that language. She could read Sophocles and Euripides in the original Greek. To an ambassador who praised her for her mastery of tongues, she replied that it was easy enough to teach a woman to speak; the difficult thing was to teach her to be silent.

duct) was directly related to his magnificence and to his talent for showmanship. Her subjects were avid for spectacles, and Elizabeth did not disappoint them. But unlike her father she was opposed to extravagance, and preferred, whenever possible, to use someone else's money. Her state officials knew something of this. The struggle they had to be reimbursed for expenses incurred was such that they often ended by footing the bills themselves. But when it came to dazzling some visiting foreign dignitary, the Queen did not count the costs. The splendid palaces, built or embellished by Henry VIII—Greenwich, Windsor, Nonesuch, Richmond and all the others up and down the Thames which the King had appropriated—opened their majestic gates to the guests, revealing vast Italian-style gardens which had been made even more elaborate by the current taste for mythology.

In order to spare visitors the trip through the narrow and malodorous streets of London, they were wafted on barges which glided along the river to the echoes of music alternating with bursts of cannon. Hunts, balls and masquerades completed the program.

Left: Contemporary English print of a picnic in the woods. The courtiers form a circle around the Queen, who is sitting under a tree, while servants bustle about with food and drink. Scenes of this sort were a commonplace occurrence during the summer visits, when the Court moved from one stately house to another. Center: A little-known portrait of the young Elizabeth. Although she was not a beauty by accepted standards, the Queen had a singular fascination which she retained until her old age. She had dark eyes and reddish-blonde hair which in later years she covered with a wig, partly to conceal the ravages of time, partly to follow a popular fashion. Below: Queen Elizabeth hawking. This sport was very popular among the nobility, who kept skilled falconers in their retinue and read books on the art of hawking. Other favorite amusements of the Queen were dancing, which she practiced with great skill until her old age, riding, music and singing.

CLOTHING AND COSMETICS

The plain and austere clothes which Elizabeth had been obliged to wear in her youth were replaced by a wardrobe of dazzling magnificence when she ascended the throne. During her entire reign she was to remain the arbiter of elegance in a society accustomed to squandering entire patrimonies on wardrobes. The appearance of the Queen was always striking. She was covered from head to foot with jewels, especially pearls. The color of her costumes was always chosen to enhance the magnolia-like pallor of her skin and the tawny shade of her hair and, later, of her wigs. Her favorite colors for official appearances were white or black, in satin, velvet, or damask. Sometimes she was dressed in violet for a more daring contrast. Englishmen sent abroad were expected to study the new fashions and to make purchases: for example, fur muffs and collars from France, perfumed gloves from Italy. Among the novelties that thrilled the ladies of Elizabeth's entourage as well as the Queen herself were knitted stockings which fashionable ladies on the continent had been wearing but which were unknown until then in England. There the ladies, even the elegant Anne Boleyn, had always worn stockings made of cloth, sometimes taffeta, which could not be made to fit any more tightly than long gaiters. The new fashion alarmed the moralists. Loud praises were sung of one of the most austere ladies of the period, Lady Dacre, because she had never been willing to wear knitted stockings.

When Elizabeth died, her wardrobe contained no less than 300 dresses so stiff with embroidery and precious stones that they could easily have stood up unaided. This mania for elaborate dress spread also to the men. Jerkins embroidered with precious stones were part of the courtier's normal equipment. Plumes were fastened on velvet caps with a diamond or a ruby. Even the least frivolous of statesmen, like William Cecil, never appeared in public without waist-length heavy gold chains around their necks, from which hung some sort of heavy pendant. Cosmetics were widely used. The Queen had a special cream with an almond base whose secret was sought in Italy and other far-flung lands, and the fame of the whiteness of her skin had traveled as far as the Near East. The secret was not divulged.

Above: The mode of dress of a lady and a country woman shown in a late 16th-century wood engraving. At that period there were clear-cut rules for dressing. They not only described what ornaments could be worn but listed the kinds of clothes suitable for various social circles. It was thus easy to see at a glance a person's place in the social hierarchy. Fashion was set chiefly in France and in Italy. Sleeves were worn to the wrist, and skirts were long. Only at the neck was there any flesh seen. The collar was often stiff with starch and trimmed with lace.

Opposite page, above: Elizabethan dress for a lady, a maiden, a gentleman, a page. Below: Two musicians: an organist and a lute player. Men's dress of this period rivaled women's in richness and in jewelled ornamentation. Dressing was such a complicated operation that no man of quality could hope to do it unaided; he needed the help of at least two servants. Even in prisons, like the Tower of London, the assistance of domestics was permitted; on occasion they even served their masters right up to the executioner's block.

THE MARRIAGE PROBLEM

"Everything depends on the husband this woman takes," wrote the Spanish ambassador Feria at the beginning of Elizabeth's reign, and with the word "everything" he was not referring to England alone but to Europe torn by religious wars. The 25-year-old Queen was in no hurry to marry. When she was still a princess, during the reign of her sister Mary, the name of the Duke of Savoy had been put forward repeatedly. At that time he was scarcely more than a dependent of the Spanish Court. Elizabeth had declared that she did not want to marry; she repeated it when she became Queen. It would be a great satisfaction to her when she died, she said, "if a marble stone should hereafter declare that a Queen, having reigned such a time, lived and died a virgin." Naturally the Court and Parliament refused to take her seriously. There was no more pressing problem than that of royal succession. Were Elizabeth to die without having an heir, the very independence of the country and the Anglican religion would be in jeopardy. In fact, the crown came to be claimed, not without justification, by another grandchild of Henry VII, Mary Stuart, Queen of Scots by right of birth and Queen of France by marriage; in other words, a foreigner, and furthermore, a Catholic. Mary had already added to her coat-of-arms those of the English ruling house which made quite plain what her intentions were. It was easy, therefore, to understand the insistence with which the House of Lords and the House of Commons begged Elizabeth to make up her mind. An unexpected illness or an assassin's stroke might well mean the end of England in addition to the Queen. But the years passed, and Elizabeth persisted in her strange reluctance. In 1566 Parliament actually threatened to block her subsidies unless the question of matrimony was immediately settled. Her reply, uttered as always with disarming candor, was: "I say again, I will marry as soon as I can conveniently, if God take not away him whom I mind to marry, or myself, or else some other great (hindrance) happen. . . . And I hope to have children, otherwise I would never marry." The tone of sincerity was such that the Council retired convinced as usual that they had taken a definite step forward. Then everything went on exactly as it had before.

*Above, left: Lord
Cumberland, richly appareled.
Right: The poet Sir Philip Sidney
and his brother Robert.
They were the sons of Edward
VI's favorite companion, Sir
Henry Sidney. The two
youths enjoyed the favor of Queen
Elizabeth whose praises Sir
Philip sang in his poetry. The
poet died prematurely at the
battle of Zutphen in Flanders.
Left: Two other Elizabethan
poets: Edmund Spenser reading an
ode to Sir Walter Raleigh.*

LEICESTER: THE GYPSY

According to some contemporaries, Elizabeth's reluctance to marry was because of Robert Dudley, later Earl of Leicester. They were the same age and old playmates at the court of Henry VIII. He was one of the first to pay homage to her on the day she became Queen, arriving suddenly, like a knight on a charger, among the groups of new courtiers. An account says that he was riding a snow-white steed; his good looks, his height and his blooming youth made him stand out. Elizabeth appointed him, on the spot, Master of the Horse. On the day of the coronation, Dudley rode beside the royal coach; in the royal palace an apartment was assigned to him next to Her Majesty's. Gossip soon spread, eagerly reported by foreign ambassadors. The Queen seemed to enjoy fanning it with disconcerting statements to the effect that Lord Robert was the most perfect man she knew. The courtiers hated him. He was nicknamed "the Gypsy," whether from his swarthy complexion or from the tribe of adventurers and vagabonds from which he stemmed. His father had died on the block, his grandfather also; the latter accused of extortion, the former of high treason. Dudley had a wife, Amy Robsart, whom he neglected. She was beautiful and rather stupid and lived in a castle in the country. On a September day in 1560, the startling news quickly spread that Amy had been found dead, her neck broken, at the foot of a flight of stairs. Accident or crime, no one will ever know, but public opinion accused her husband. An inquest handed down a verdict of accidental death, but the rumors persisted. In France, Mary Stuart, wife of young King Francis II, made venomous comments on the "fortunate accident" which would allow her cousin to marry her "horse keeper." The marriage, however, did not take place, then or later. Perhaps those who saw the bond between the Queen and Dudley as something other than a lovers' bond were right. They were bound together by a spiritual affinity which had sprung up during their childhood (they were born on the same day, at the same hour); this was strengthened in their youth when they were both imprisoned in the Tower. But whatever the basis of their relationship, it lasted until Leicester's death in 1588.

THE
Compleat Ambaſſador:
or two
Treaties of the intended marriage
of Qu: Elizabeth of Glorious memory; Compriſed in
Letters of Negatiation of Sr Fra: Walſingham (her Reſi-
dent in France) together with the Anſwers of the
Lord Burleigh, the Earle of Leiceſter, Sr Thomas
Smith, and others.
Faythfully Collected by the truly Honourable,
Sr Dudley Diggs Kt late Mr of the Rolls.

Sold by Ga: Bedell, and Tho: Collins,
at the Middle Temple Gate:
1655.

ADULATION
AND LOYALTY

Mary Stuart differed from Elizabeth in one important respect: her ability to evaluate men. A very poor judge of character, always spurred by the blind impulses of passion or caprice, Mary invariably chose the worst person at the worst time. Elizabeth was equally emotional, but the difficult years of her childhood had taught her self-control. It had been a hard school, but she learned from it. Passions were not alien to her, but her mind remained clear; she had ample opportunity to prove this during various crises in her life as woman and as Queen. Her advisers were not chosen from among her favorites or from among the courtiers who called her the "Faerie Queen" and who celebrated her beauty with extravagant praise. They were picked from the new middle class, which was henceforth to make up the backbone of the nation, rather than from the feudal aristocracy which centuries of privilege had weakened. Her choices included merchants, businessmen, country squires, a whole hard-bitten tribe of social climbers and fortune builders with hearty appetites and hard heads. The

Queen herself, through her mother, belonged to this class. The Boleyn family fortune did not originate with the crusades but in the dark shop of a grandfather who was a silk and wool merchant. His descendants tried to obliterate these humble beginnings, but Elizabeth probably remembered. In any event, support of the middle classes was in the tradition of the House of Tudor. Elizabeth pursued the same course as had her father and his father. Her secretary of State, William Cecil, later Lord Burghley, who remained by her side for 40 years, came from a family of modest social status which had been enriched by the distribution of abbey lands and wealth, by Henry VIII. Elizabeth told Cecil when she became Queen that she knew he would remain faithful to the State. This was what she demanded of her advisers. From her courtiers she demanded adulation as a right, but from her advisers she accepted even the most painful truths, and Cecil never spared her. The Queen and Cecil came to present such a unified front that it was to be said of Elizabeth that she was both man and woman.

Left: Two scenes in Elizabethan daily life: a night watchman, armed with a lantern and a bell, making his rounds, and a nobleman giving alms to a beggar. Below, both pages: Visscher's famous map of London, done in the 17th century, showing the Thames and London Bridge.

Left: The Royal Exchange in London. The London stock market was founded by Sir Thomas Gresham (1519–1579), the son of a merchant who had been knighted by Henry VIII. Sir Thomas offered to construct, at his own expense, a building for the Exchange, provided that a suitable location was given. This proved to be an important and profitable business. As a matter of fact, with just the rentals collected from the shops on the ground floor of the building, he more than repaid himself for his expenses.

27

MARIA

G

SCOTIA
SIMA REGINA
ANCLÆ DOTARIA
ANNO
ÆTATISREGNIQ
36
ANGLICÆ CAPTIVIT
IO
S H
1573

FEMININE SKIRMISHES AND QUEENLY RIVALRIES

In 1560 the King of France, Francis II, died of tuberculosis, or some said, of poison. He was only 17. His youthful widow, Mary Stuart, was obliged to return to her Scottish Kingdom. Permission to cross English soil was denied because she had had the effrontery to place on her coat-of-arms those of England—an act tantamount to proclaiming herself the legitimate English sovereign. This was the beginning of a duel between the two Queens that was to last almost 30 years. It was a typically feminine duel fought with barbed compliments, malicious remarks and retaliatory gossip. One day Elizabeth asked Melville, the Scottish envoy, if his sovereign was as tall as she. He replied that Mary was taller. Elizabeth retorted that Mary was too tall. For she, Elizabeth, was just the right height. Another time Elizabeth asked if Mary was a good musician. Melville replied that she played "reasonably well for a queen." Elizabeth immediately went to her favorite instrument, the virginal, and sang and played for the ambassador, displaying great talent. Then she danced—an art in which she was accomplished—with such grace that the ambassador was quite charmed. But the real causes of the rivalry went deeper than these skirmishes. Mary was a danger to the peace of England. If the decree that had stamped Elizabeth illegitimate was accepted, the throne would go to Mary Stuart, the legitimate granddaughter of Henry VII. Because of this, she was a formidable tool in the hands of the Catholic powers and of the English dissidents. But unfortunately for herself and for her supporters, she was very unpopular—in fact she was hated by her subjects for her scandalous conduct. Her only qualities—beauty and courage—were not enough to cancel her enormous blunders and her complete lack of scruples. Her marriage to Lord Darnley, a stupid, long-legged blond boy, aroused violently hostile reactions in Scotland; these became more marked after the barbarous assassination of her musician-secretary, the Italian David Rizzio, by the instigation of her consort. Three months after the death of Rizzio, on June 19, 1566, at Edinburgh Castle, Mary gave birth to a son, the future James VI of Scotland. It was whispered that he would certainly be as wise as Solomon because, like the Biblical King, he was the son of David who played the harp.

Opposite page: Mary, Queen of Scots, in the famous portrait at the National Gallery in London. At every period of her life the Queen was a favorite subject for painters and poets. She herself enjoyed music and poetry, but her verses in French were amateurish and uninspired. Above left: Portrait of

Marie de Guise, wife of James V of Scotland and mother of Mary Stuart. Above right: Portrait of Mary Stuart's infant son, James, who was to unite the kingdoms of Scotland and England. Below: Mary Stuart, in her youth, with her first husband, Francis II, King of France.

LOVES, IMPRISONMENTS AND
PLOTS OF THE QUEEN OF SCOTS

Mary Stuart's second husband, Henry, Lord Darnley, was not destined to live long. The Queen tired of him a few months after their marriage, and the Rizzio incident did nothing to help their relationship. However, before resorting to drastic solutions, it was essential that her son James—acknowledged by Darnley as being his—be christened. The Queen of England was asked to become godmother. Elizabeth, who was represented by a proxy, sent a magnificent present: a baptismal font of enamelled gold. Meanwhile, relations between the royal couple deteriorated rapidly, and the unfortunate Darnley spoke of leaving the country. Shortly thereafter a mysterious explosion destroyed the house where Darnley was recovering from smallpox. His body was found in the garden; he had apparently been strangled. Three months later the Queen married the Earl of Bothwell, the most unpopular of her noblemen, who was strongly suspected of having been, with her connivance, the instigator of Darnley's murder. Public opinion reacted violently against this ill-omened marriage. Mary, hated by her subjects and attacked by her rebellious nobles, was obliged to abdicate in favor of her young son. Bothwell did not hesitate to abandon her; in Edinburgh, where she was taken as a prisoner, the crowds shouted, "Burn the whore!" She was held under surveillance at Lochleven Castle while her subjects cried out for her execution. (They would have carried it out had it not been for Elizabeth, who feared that the spectacle of a Queen executed by her subjects would be a damaging one.) The imprisonment lasted 10 months, and Mary devoted the time to plotting her escape. In May 1568 she succeeded and sought asylum on English soil. Her presence in England, which was bound to bring trouble, alarmed Elizabeth's ministers. According to them, the only way to get rid of Mary was to have her beheaded, a course of action they thought was amply justified by the results of Darnley's inquest. Elizabeth, as was her wont, compromised. The exiled Queen would be imprisoned with all the honors and considerations due her rank. All things being equal, this was a fair decision, but it did not mean that Mary would be content to live in peace. For almost 20 years she was the moving spirit of every plot against Elizabeth.

Opposite page: Two 19th-century prints showing scenes in Mary's tumultuous life. In the first, the young Queen disembarks in Scotland, having been widowed at 18 by the death of Francis II of Valois, eldest son of Catherine de Medici. In the second, Mary is shown at the Castle of Lochleven where she was held prisoner after having signed her abdication.

Above: Another 19th-century print shows Mary protesting against the commission that was to judge her.
Left: The murder of the Queen's musician-secretary, the Italian David Rizzio, at Holyrood Castle near Edinburgh on March 9, 1566, in the hall where he had been dining with the Queen and the Countess of Argyll. Henry Darnley broke into the room with a group of conspirators, all enemies of Rizzio's because of the favors the Italian was constantly receiving from the Queen. Later, 56 stab wounds were counted on the body of the hapless victim.

MARY STUART'S COURAGE ON THE BATTLEFIELD

Above: A 19th-century etching of Mary Stuart. Typical of her reactions was the following episode which took place in a house in Edinburgh one day. During a discussion about the likeness of a portrait of the Queen of England, namely Elizabeth, Mary Stuart cut short the discussion by saying, "Nay, it is not like her, for I am Queen of England." Indeed she always claimed to be, basing this on her descent from Margaret Tudor, sister of Henry VIII.
Right: Fattori's painting of Mary Stuart on the field of battle. She was often at war against her subjects and against the rebellious nobles of Scotland, until her forces were put to flight at Carberry Hill. Even Bothwell, her third husband, abandoned her to her fate. When she was taken back to Edinburgh, the crowds wanted to send her to the stake.

On these two pages are scenes from the bloody Wars of Religion which plunged France into mourning during the reigns of the last Valois.
Near right: The assassination of Henri, Duc de Guise. This powerful noble, of the house of Lorraine, was the leader and guiding spirit of the Catholic extremists during the Wars of Religion. He was in great part responsible for the Massacre of St. Bartholomew's Day. He was killed in the Chateau de Blois in 1588 by order of Henry III.
Far right: The death of Admiral Coligny, the most influential of the Huguenots or French Protestants. The admiral was murdered in his own house.
Below: Scene showing the massacre of August 24, 1572, St. Bartholomew's Day. Historians disagree on the total number of victims, but there must have been thousands. The massacre, begun in the capital, spread to the provinces despite royal orders to have it stopped.

THE SHADOW OF ST. BARTHOLOMEW'S NIGHT

When Elizabeth came to the throne, she adopted a religious policy that was exceptionally tolerant. Despite her two predecessors' religious mania, she steered as steady a course as was feasible, in an era given to frenzied religious persecution, between Catholic fanaticism and Puritan bigotry. "Let it not be said that *our* reformation tended to cruelty," she exclaimed. She had prayed to God to enable her to reign without shedding blood. Later she was not always able to follow her program of clemency, because of circumstances (chief among them the Pope's Bull of Excommunication against her) and pressure from her ministers, who saw in the activity of the Catholics a threat to the State. But her abhorrence of death sentences was genuine, probably rooted in tragic childhood reminiscences. Fourteen years were to pass before the daughter of the beheaded Anne Boleyn could bring herself to sign a warrant for a beheading—that of the Duke of Norfolk, guilty of having conspired with Mary Stuart to place the latter on the throne of England. And even in this case the Queen was so reluctant that she postponed it from February to June of 1572 while the chief instigator was spared. The executioner's block at the top of the Tower had so long lain idle that it had rotted and was falling to pieces, and a new one had to be provided for Norfolk. Elizabeth's moderation was far from being shared by her advisers. The most resolute in the opposition was Cecil's son-in-law, Sir Francis Walsingham. In that same year, 1572, when Walsingham was ambassador to the French Court, he was an eyewitness to the slaughter of St. Bartholomew's Day, the darkest page in the whole history of religious conflict in France. The facts were as follows: At daybreak of August 24, 1572, partisans of the Duc de Guise— the Catholic extremists—with the secret connivance of Catherine de' Medici and King Charles IX, at a given signal, started slaughtering Protestants. In Paris alone the victims, taken by surprise, numbered about 2,000. The effect on England was profound. The French Ambassador Fénelon, admitted into Windsor after four days of waiting, crossed one antechamber after another filled with silent courtiers dressed in mourning, before he reached the Presence Chamber. There the Queen heaped passionate reproaches on him. The searing memory of the night of St. Bartholomew doubtless made Elizabeth's advisers both wary and fierce, and more than ever determined to fight Mary Stuart and the Catholics.

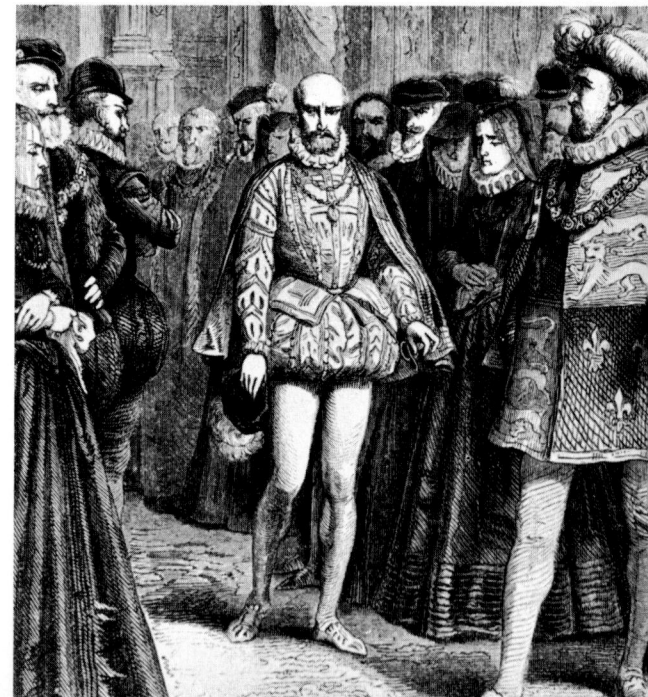

Above: A ball at the court of Henry III depicted in a painting of a 16th-century French school. Despite the violent convulsions of civil and religious struggles, the French court during the reigns of the last Valois Kings was bathed in splendor. Henry III, who succeeded his brothers Francis II and Charles IX, was something of a dandy. One evening he appeared at a court function wearing a suit of white satin on which were embroidered the lines of a love poem punctuated with precious stones.

Right: A 19th-century print showing the reception accorded the French ambassador to the English Court, de la Mothe Fénelon, after the massacre of the Huguenots in 1572. The mourning clothes of the onlookers and their sorrowful expressions proclaim the general gloom. Fénelon tried to defend the Queen Mother, Catherine de' Medici, and her son Charles IX, by asserting that discovery of a Protestant conspiracy had necessitated severe reprisals.
Opposite page:
Catherine de' Medici.

RELATIONS
WITH FRANCE

Not only at the time of the night of St. Bartholomew but during every moment of the reign of Elizabeth, relations with France of the Valois were strained and uncertain. The hostility between the two countries went back for centuries. It was said in Elizabethan times that when the Ethiopians turned white, the French would love the English. The Tudors had based their foreign policy on the clever game of the balance of power between the two rival nations, France and Spain. Then, Mary Tudor destroyed this balance by throwing herself, literally as well as figuratively, into the arms of Spain, personified by her consort, Philip. The consequence of this alliance, matrimonial and political, was not long in coming: Caught in a ruinous war against the French, England had to give up Calais, her last foothold on the continent. That the Stuarts were doubly bound to French fortune, no one doubted: Mary Stuart's mother, Marie de Guise, who was regent in her name for a long time, belonged to the powerful house of Lorraine which headed the Catholic extremists. But popular sentiment in Scotland was violently opposed to them, in the name of Protestantism and nationalism. Elizabeth capitalized on these two forces to fan covertly but effectively the anti-Stuart "guerrilla" warfare. Later, when Mary was only a prisoner and her young son James was being brought up in the Protestant faith, the French peril continued. France, too, was governed by a woman— Catherine de' Medici—although nominally the power rested in the hands of her sons. In rapid succession they succeeded each other on the throne, but were killed off by some of the Valois hereditary diseases. Every so often "Madame Catherine" proposed one of them as a husband for Elizabeth: first Charles IX, then Henry III, finally her youngest, the Duc d'Alençon. It was as good a way as any to put her hand on English gold and English soil. Elizabeth didn't say "no"; this would have been against her principles. On the contrary, she encouraged the beginnings of the negotiations. Even when the motive was openly political, nothing appealed more to the Queen than being courted, and nothing repelled her more than its logical conclusion.

MARRIAGE = DEATH

Left: Thomas Howard, Duke of Norfolk, portrayed in a print made in 1577. One of the foremost peers of England, he rebelled against Queen Elizabeth for the sake of Mary Stuart. He was executed in 1572. His poet father, the Count of Surrey, had met a similar end in 1547 for having rebelled against Henry VIII.

It is often said that the reason for Elizabeth's aversion to marriage must have been a physical disability which would have prevented her from childbearing. In support of this thesis are the words the Queen uttered upon learning of the birth of James Stuart: "The Queen of Scots is lighter of a fair son, and I am but a barren stock!" However, the only proof of the authenticity of this outburst was the word of the Scottish ambassador. Actually, the court doctors twice examined Elizabeth in view of matrimonial plans and declared that she could certainly bear children. One of the reasons for her reluctance to marry may have been because she had undertaken the burden of governing in an era when reigning Queens were a rarity. Today the tendency is to ascribe the reason as not a physical disability but a psychological one; the roots of which went back to her infancy, a neglected and insecure one. Twice the executioner's axe was used to solve Henry VIII's conjugal problems. Of the tragic end of her mother Anne Boleyn, accused of adultery, Elizabeth could have no direct memory for she was not yet three at the time; but some echo of it must have reached her, amplified and rendered even more frightening by the nameless terrors which surround children left to their own devices. She was eight years old when the tragedy was repeated, the protagonist this time being 20-year-old Catherine Howard, Anne Boleyn's cousin and the King's fifth wife. The comment of Elizabeth's great favorite, Robert Dudley, Earl of Leicester, seems particularly illuminating: "I have known her since she was eight years of age, better than any man in the world. From that time she has always, invariably, declared that she would remain unmarried." The coincidence of dates speaks for itself. Furthermore, Elizabeth's first known suitor, Admiral Thomas Seymour, who was so attentive to the 14-year-old orphan, also ended by losing his head on the block; one of the accusations directed against him was that he had aspired to the hand of a royal princess without permission from the Royal Council. And so for the third time, in those difficult years of adolescence, the idea of marriage appeared to her bound to the idea of death by the axe. It was a psychological trauma which was never to be dispelled.

Opposite page, below: Portrait of Nicholas Bacon. Keeper of the Great Seal of England, Sir Nicholas was also the brother-in-law of Elizabeth's minister, William Cecil. His two sons, Anthony and Francis, distinguished themselves in the second half of Elizabeth's reign, the elder as jurist and the younger as philosopher, statesman and essayist. Left: The Queen receiving young Francis Bacon (later Lord Verulam) at Court. Below left: Elizabeth watching a celebration. Directly below: Portrait of Sir Walter Raleigh. He had fallen in disgrace and been sent to the Tower for having compromised young Bess Throckmorton, one of the Queen's ladies-in-waiting, whom he later married.

39

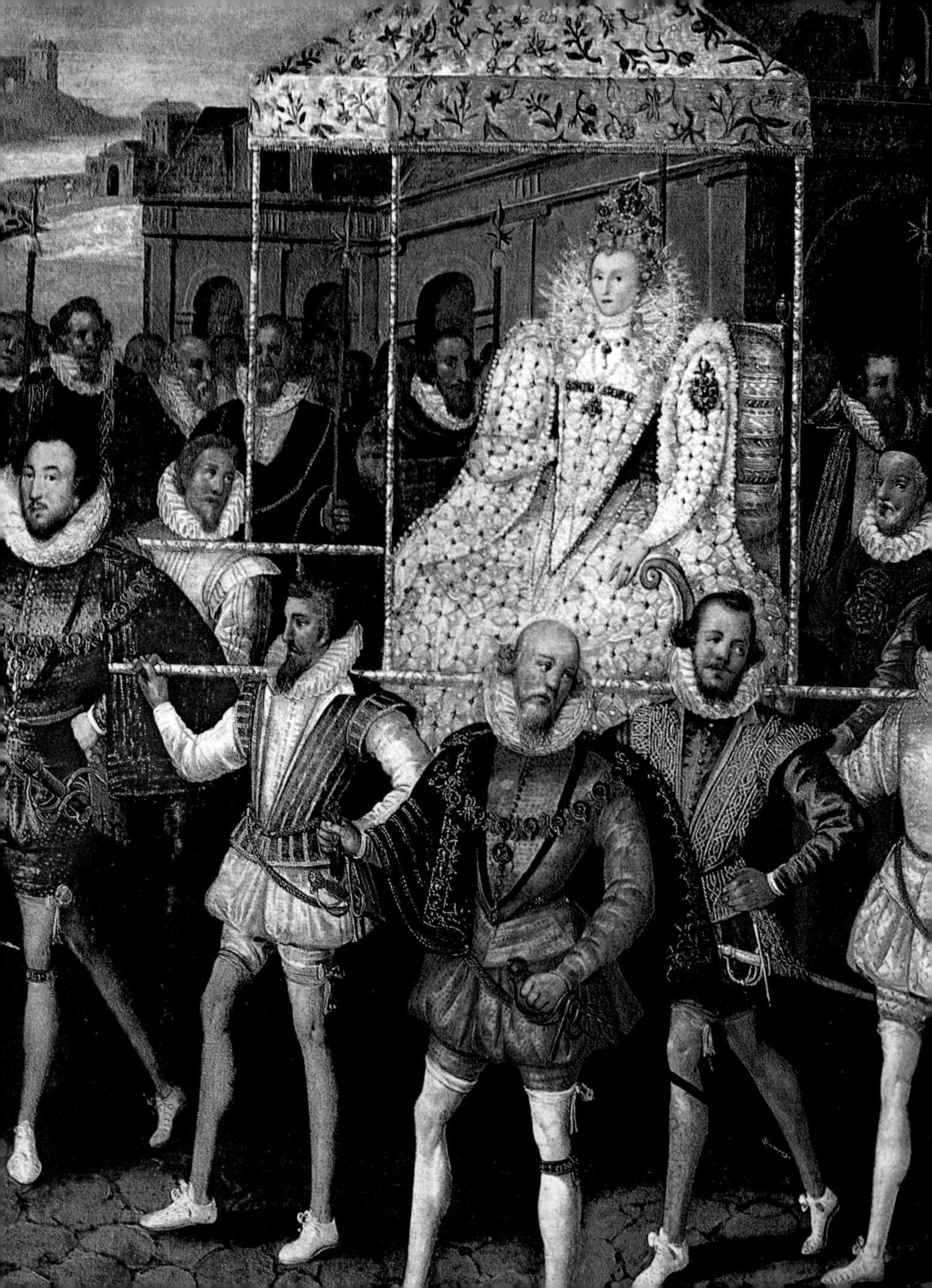

ENGLAND, HER ONLY LOVE

Opposite page: A portrait, by the Dutch painter Marcus Gheeraerts, of Queen Elizabeth at Blackfriars surrounded by her guard of honor. Her characteristic pose of an "earthly idol," which she assumed toward the end of her reign, is apparent here. The sumptuous fashions of the period greatly contributed to this mystique.
Below: Richmond Palace toward the end of the 16th century. Henry VII (the Earl of Richmond) took over Shene Palace, rebuilt it and renamed it.
Below, right: Niccolò dell'Abate's painting, at the Este Gallery in Modena, shows one means of transportation in the 16th century.

Elizabeth's obscure reluctance to marriage did not however prevent her from surrounding herself with admirers to whom she granted considerable license. It was a circle of brilliant and devoted men who burned incense to her as to an idol, and whom she in turn attracted and repulsed, stirring their jealousies. She often gave them curious nicknames: Leicester was called "Eyes," Christopher Hatton, "Mutton," and Walter Raleigh, "Water." Meantime, marriage negotiations with continental princes continued. Elizabeth used these as a diplomatic weapon to build alliances or to avert the danger of war: an exquisitely feminine weapon which appealed to her because it flattered her vanity. The game often continued for years, with messages, exchanges of presents, misunderstandings, reconciliations and a great coming and going of ambassadors.

The truth was probably glimpsed by an anonymous author of popular ballads who, in 1571, represented the sovereign as a marriageable girl named Bessie. Her lover's name was England. To him alone had Bessie plighted her hand and her troth: "Here is my hand, my dear lover England!" run the words of the song.

CATHOLIC MARTYRDOM: POLITICAL RATHER THAN RELIGIOUS

The hostility between the Queen and the Catholics had been fanned by an uprising, in 1570, of the northern counties. Because of it, Mary Stuart had to be hurriedly transferred from Tutbury Castle to Coventry. The insurrection was swiftly quelled, but in the course of it Pope Clement V issued a Bull of Excommunication against Elizabeth. A copy of this document was found pinned to the door of the Bishop of London's house on the morning of May 1, 1570. The Bull had a political as well as religious significance in that it released English Catholic subjects from loyalty to the Crown. Its immediate effect was to render suspect the loyalty of all Elizabeth's Catholic subjects and to reinforce the Protestants' hand against them. That the persecutions were essentially political was conceded by the Catholics themselves at the time. One of them, Allen, wrote: "The question is not about religion, of which our enemies have not one bit; but about the stability of the kingdom, about worldly prosperity." Many of those arrested were priests educated in foreign seminaries for the purpose of bringing England back into the Catholic fold. There was a seminary in Douai, in Flanders, which was in operation in 1568; another one was opened in Rome in 1579 by the Jesuits. This one was later called the Seminary of Martyrs, because of the fate that awaited many of its pupils. One of these was the noble and courageous Edmund Campion, whom Elizabeth remembered as a student at Oxford and whom, after his capture, she tried to help by offering him one loophole after another. Asked if he thought the Pope might lawfully depose her, Campion replied evasively. To the question of what he would do if the Pope sent an army to dethrone her, his reply was: "I would do as God should give me grace." After that it was difficult even for the Queen to save him. Nonetheless she persisted. A simple concession to the Anglican service would have sufficed, but in his eyes this would have been tantamount to betraying the ideals of his whole life. Torture and the horrible death reserved for traitors awaited him—being drawn and quartered in public. A great many Catholics died in this fashion, just as a great many Protestants had been burned at the stake. A "person in authority" at last granted Campion a gesture of mercy. He was to be allowed to hang until he was dead instead of being disembowelled alive.

Above and opposite page: Arrest and martyrdom of English Catholics shown in 16th and 17th-century engravings. The persecutions took place during the second half of Elizabeth's reign when the Queen, goaded by her ministers, adopted a policy of force. In this manner, 128 priests—a great many of them Jesuits—58 laymen and 3 women (according to a contemporary Catholic source) perished. Besides these, 32 Franciscan monks were allowed to die of hunger in prison. Among the most famous victims were Campion, whom even Lord Burghley had referred to as the "jewel of England," and Robert Southwell, who underwent such barbaric torture that the Protestants themselves were appalled.

THE PURITANS: THE OTHER EXTREME

Catholics did not provide the only opposition to Elizabeth's domestic policy. With the passage of time, another hostile group came into being, this one from the extreme wing of the Protestant faction. They were the followers of Calvin, the most inflexible of the reformers. He carried Luther's precepts to extremes by doing away with the traditional ecclesiastic hierarchy, the sacraments, and the outward forms of worship. In Geneva he established a community in which the faithful elected a synod consisting of ministers and elders to oversee the church service, and to give assistance to the poor and to the sick. Rigidly based on the theory of predestination and the doctrine of Luther, Calvinism spread rapidly in Europe in the second half of the 16th century. In France the Huguenots came into being, in Scotland the Presbyterians, in England the Puritans, thus named because of their program to purify the English Church of the last remains of "popism." These groups had different characteristics, but their common tendency toward a democratic order made them suspect to governments; it also assured them a large following, especially from the mercantile middle classes in urban centers. In England, the monarchy considered them, paradoxically, as offensive as the Catholics. Elizabeth looked upon the Puritans as a grave danger to the security of the State. They were already extensively represented in Parliament. What particularly infuriated the Queen was their smugness. Francis Bacon, the philosopher, wrote of the Puritans that "they have but two small wants: knowledge and love." And indeed there was something glacial in their pride, their refusal of joy, their somber boasting of being the elect. They looked upon others as children of perdition, idolaters, sons of Belial.

Opposite page: Portrait of John Foxe, the Protestant writer who in his Book of Martyrs collected the stories of the sufferings of his fellow Protestants at the time of Mary Tudor. This book, placed next to the Bible in many English houses, contributed to perpetuating the name of Elizabeth's half sister as "Bloody Mary."

Directly below: Satirized picture of the Catholic church in a 16th-century etching. Protestant propaganda, based on examples of churchly corruption in certain Renaissance circles, represented Rome as the seat of superstition and of every conceivable vice. To them "popism" was synonymous with "idolatry." Bottom of page, left:

The frontispiece of the prayer book used by Elizabeth. Right: Puritans about to emigrate from England. Departures of this sort, motivated by a desire for religious freedom, grew in number during the reign of Elizabeth's successor, James I, and contributed to the colonization of North America.

DRAKE

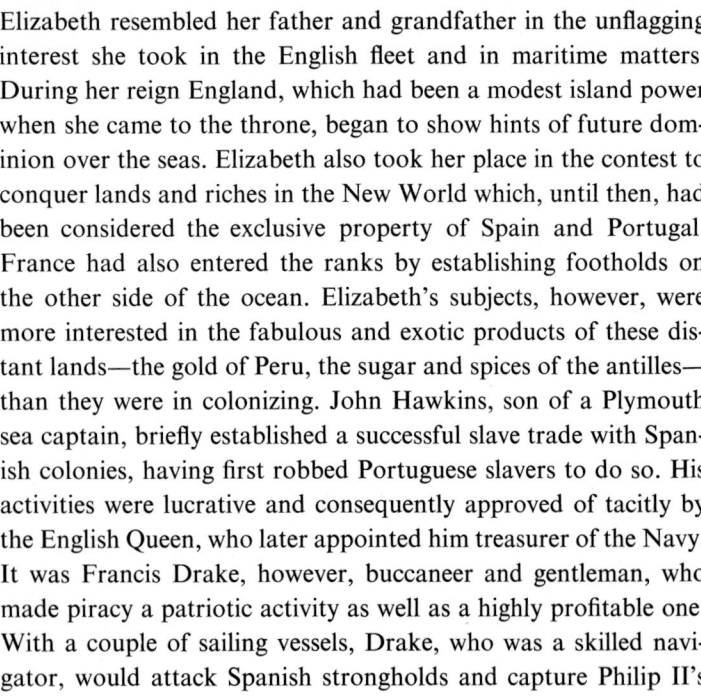

Elizabeth resembled her father and grandfather in the unflagging interest she took in the English fleet and in maritime matters. During her reign England, which had been a modest island power when she came to the throne, began to show hints of future dominion over the seas. Elizabeth also took her place in the contest to conquer lands and riches in the New World which, until then, had been considered the exclusive property of Spain and Portugal. France had also entered the ranks by establishing footholds on the other side of the ocean. Elizabeth's subjects, however, were more interested in the fabulous and exotic products of these distant lands—the gold of Peru, the sugar and spices of the antilles—than they were in colonizing. John Hawkins, son of a Plymouth sea captain, briefly established a successful slave trade with Spanish colonies, having first robbed Portuguese slavers to do so. His activities were lucrative and consequently approved of tacitly by the English Queen, who later appointed him treasurer of the Navy. It was Francis Drake, however, buccaneer and gentleman, who made piracy a patriotic activity as well as a highly profitable one. With a couple of sailing vessels, Drake, who was a skilled navigator, would attack Spanish strongholds and capture Philip II's

galleons. On returning to his native land, he would be greeted with secret letters of congratulations from the Queen and official messages of reproof because it was not "correct" to attack the bases of a country with which one was not at war. Elizabeth, furthermore, lost no time in claiming her share of the booty. Drake's most glorious undertaking took place in 1577 and finished in 1580. It was the first circumnavigation of the globe since Magellan's. Added to the geographic merit of the undertaking were tangible advantages, for Drake had sacked, en route, many Spanish ports and islands, not to mention rival galleons. One of these, taken by surprise between Lima and Panama, was laden with gold, silver, and emeralds from Peru. The booty amounted to more than the income of the English crown for one entire year. The Queen, accompanied by the French ambassador, went to Deptford to visit Drake's ship. She gaily told Drake that she had a sword to cut off his head. Actually, the sword was used to knight him. Drake, on his knees, heard from the lips of Elizabeth, "Rise, Sir Francis." The French envoy enthusiastically embraced the man whom the Spaniards would have liked to see on the gallows.

Opposite page: John Hawkins (left) and Francis Drake, two outstanding figures during the initial period of English power on the seas. Hawkins' plundering of Portuguese ships and administrative talent did much to boost the supremacy of the English Navy. Directly below, left: The Queen knighting Francis Drake. Bottom of page, left: Drake's wife, Elizabeth Sydenham. Below, right: This 19th-century print shows Elizabeth on board Drake's ship. From the booty taken from the Spaniards, Drake picked out 5 enormous emeralds and a quantity of diamonds which he had set into a superb crown. He gave the crown as a present to the Queen at the New Year's celebrations of 1581. Two court officials, Lord Burghley and Lord Sussex, refused Drake's offering (10 ingots of gold and a gold dinner service for each), saying indignantly that these were stolen goods—or so the Spanish ambassador reported.

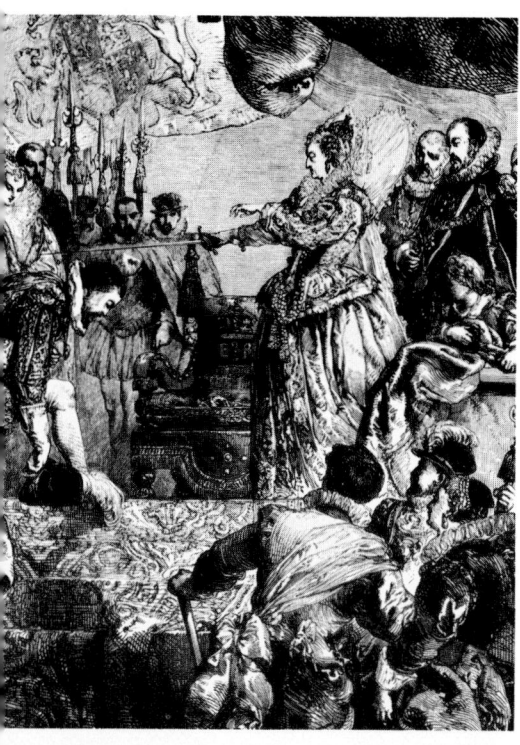

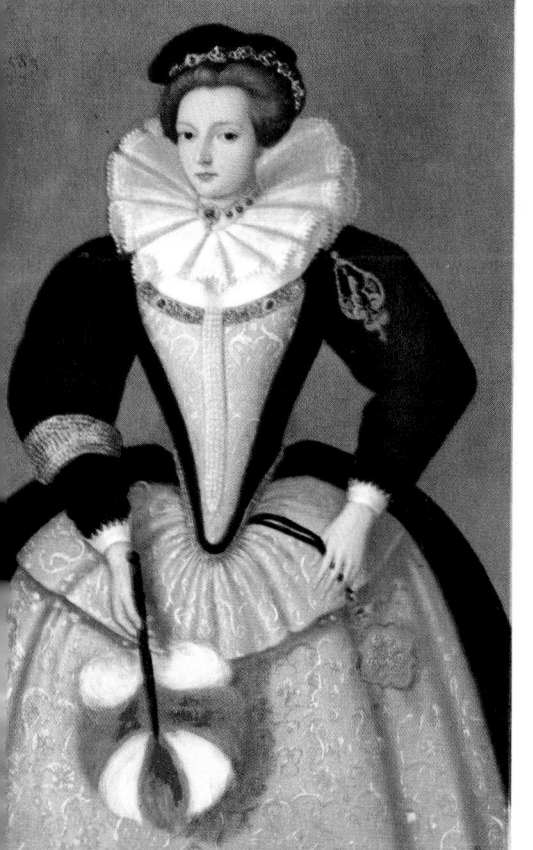

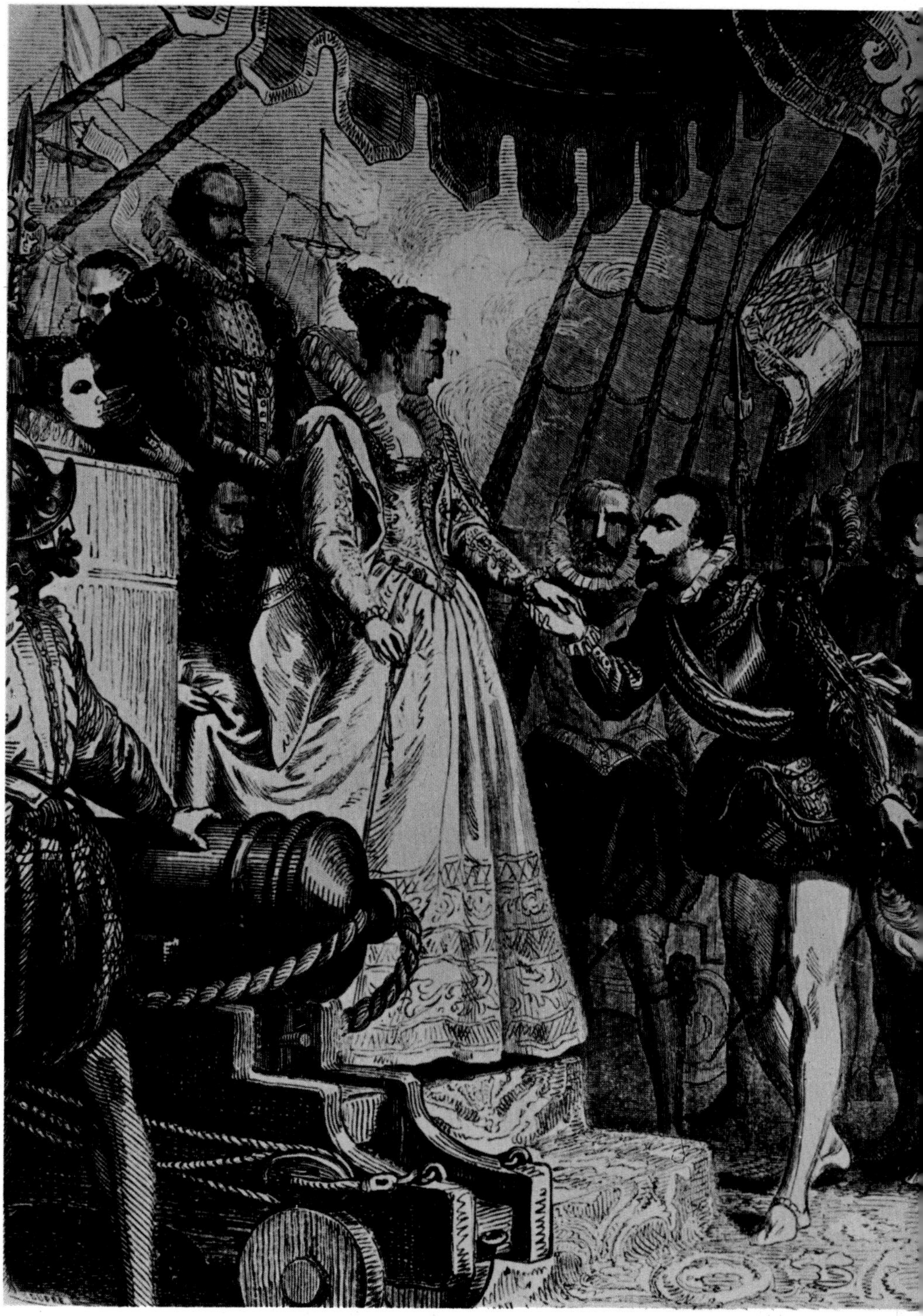

VIRGINIA: TO HONOR THE VIRGIN QUEEN

Opposite page: Adam Willaerts's oil painting at the Naval Museum in Greenwich, England, of a ship of the East India Company setting sail from an English port in the early 17th century. Below left: An etching by de Bry done in 1599, of the marketplace at Goa. It was a period in which England's interest in overseas territory was livelier than ever. Below: Virginia natives and Indian warriors of the same region at the time of the early English settlements. These pictures were done by John White, the first governor of the English Colony at the time of Raleigh.

The creation of a British Empire overseas was made possible by Sir Walter Raleigh and his half-brother, Sir Humphrey Gilbert. To the latter the Queen granted as early as 1578 the authority to colonize "remote and barbarous lands" not yet in the possession of any prince in Christendom. But Gilbert's expedition came to an unlucky end. After landing on Newfoundland, the small ships, already buffeted about by numerous storms, were caught in a hurricane. Gilbert lost his life, and the royal letters patent were transferred to Walter Raleigh. He was to be the spiritual and financial backer of successive expeditions, although he himself took no direct part in any of them until 1595. The first voyage took place in 1584: two vessels set sail from England on April 27 and on July 13 anchored near an island off what is today the North Carolina coast. The descriptions of the region, given by the returning men, were enthusiastic. Two natives, exhibited as a "curiosity," had consented to accompany them back to England. In honor of Elizabeth, celebrated at court as the "Virgin Queen," the land across the ocean was named Virginia. The success of this voyage of exploration encouraged Raleigh to found a real colony. The first attempt, in 1585, was not successful. The settlers, after a harsh winter on the island of Roanoke, sorely tried by hunger, asked Sir Francis Drake, who had arrived with his fleet, to be taken back home. The second expedition, in 1587, brought the artisans: masons, carpenters, mechanics, blacksmiths required for a colony, and 17 women and 9 children, all under the leadership of a civilian governor, the painter and water colorist John White, a veteran of the first expedition. He had 12 advisers to help him. His granddaughter, Virginia Dare, born on August 18, 1587, was the first English child born in America. After 1587 the mystery began. The supply ships which landed in Roanoke four years later (the war with Spain postponed their arrival) found the village intact but deserted and overgrown with grass and weeds. There was no trace of the little colony.

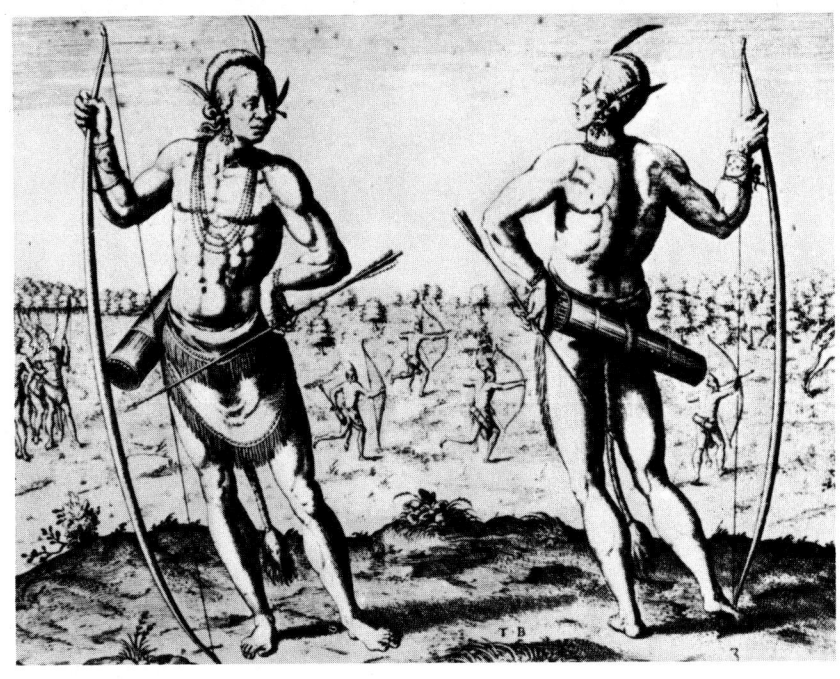

RISE OF THE GREAT MERCHANT COMPANIES

The 16th century saw the establishment in England of the great chartered companies. They were corporations which achieved trade monopoly in certain defined regions. Among the most important were the Merchant Adventurers, a group formed to monopolize trade on the large German rivers. Soon others went to the Levant, Russia, the Baltic, etc. The principal shareholders of the companies were merchants and armorers, but soon the lure of large profits attracted the peerage, the landed gentry and even the Crown. The East India Company, founded toward the end of Elizabeth's reign, obtained the monopoly for trade with Asiatic, African, and American ports.

At that time, as a consequence of Columbus's error, the name "India" indicated the new lands discovered on the other side of the Atlantic. The Company maintained control of India with its own officials until the rebellion of 1857. The active interest of the Tudor monarchs in the Navy was one of the principal causes for the rise and development of these commercial enterprises.

Right: Painting in the Naval Museum of Greenwich by the Flemish artist Andries Van Veertveld of the arrival in Amsterdam of ships of the East India Company on May 1, 1599.

ANOTHER BETROTHAL CANCELED

In 1578, when Elizabeth was 45, her aversion to matrimony appeared to be fading. A rumor spread throughout Europe that the Queen was betrothed. Her fiancé this time was Catherine de'Medici's youngest son, Prince François de Valois, Duc d'Alençon, who was barely 20. Negotiations of this kind were nothing new between Elizabeth and the French royal house. One after the other the Queen mother had proposed her sons: Charles IX, Henry III, and now the Duc d'Alençon. Because of his passion for intrigues and duplicity, the entire French court would have been delighted to see him emigrate. Therefore the invitation from London for an official visit could not have been more welcome. Motives both political and emotional spurred Elizabeth: the eternal rivalry with Spain (Alençon promised to support the Protestants in Flanders against Philip II), the need to counterbalance Mary Stuart's continuing influence, and a furious quarrel with her favorite, Leicester, provoked by her discovery of his secret marriage. Her suitor arrived in London on August 16, 1519. He was small, ugly, sickly and pockmarked, but in his pocket he brought a superb diamond, sent by "Madame Catherine" as an engagement ring. He was immediately nicknamed "the Frog." To the general astonishment, the Queen and "the Frog" appeared to be greatly taken with each other. Elizabeth said she found him less ugly than she had been led to believe. As for Alençon, he seemed to see nothing extraordinary in courting a lady twice his age. After all, he came by it honestly. His father, Henry II, had spent the best years of his youth at the feet of a 50-year-old matron, Diane de Poitiers. But England viewed the wedding preparations with alarm. The most agitated groups were the Puritans, who saw in Alençon a foreigner and a Catholic, a menace incarnate. One of them, Stubbs, was condemned to have his right hand chopped off for having written a pamphlet entitled "A Gaping Gulphe wherein England is like to be swallowed." After the execution Stubbs held up his stump shouting, "God Save the Queen!" He could have spared himself the trouble. After having fulfilled its political aim, that matrimonial project ended like all the others: in nothingness.

On this page: Two aspects of the "dolce vita" at the court of the Valois. Left: A royal hunt with falcon, dogs and lances. Below: A royal ball.
The negotiations for the marriage of Elizabeth with François de Valois, Duc d'Alençon and later Duc d'Anjou, occupied the diplomatic stage of all Europe during the years 1578 to 1580.

INCORRIGIBLE CONSPIRATOR

During the 20 years of Mary Stuart's imprisonment the two Queens never saw each other face to face, though they continued to exchange letters. But this was not the only kind of correspondence in which Mary indulged. An incorrigible intriguer, she never lost touch with Elizabeth's enemies, both inside and outside the realm. She knew all the tricks of prisoners: her letters, always in code, were sent by every conceivable means—in the boots of a brewer who supplied the castle, in the diplomatic pouch of the French ambassador. As long as she could use her beauty as a weapon, Mary did so. She promised her hand to the Duke of Norfolk, who consequently died a traitor's death on the block. Later, sickly, faded, with no admirers left, she continued to intrigue, formulating plans of invasion and a Catholic restoration based on the assassination of her cousin. What is startling in the face of this mad obstinacy is not Elizabeth's harshness but her clemency. Over and over again her ministers and Parliament, keenly aware of the danger embodied in this woman of royal blood, manipulated by enemies of England, asked for her head. But Elizabeth continued to postpone Mary's execution.

Opposite page: This famous portrait of Elizabeth in her maturity is in the National Gallery in London. The dress is in the fashion prevalent in the late 16th century. Note the enormous sleeves, the skirt billowing over a farthingale, the rigidly starched collar made of priceless lace. This fashion in collars had been imported into England by the wife of the Queen's Dutch cook. At the time of her betrothal to the Duc d'Alençon, Elizabeth dazzled even the French with her elegance. The Duke was desperate at losing her. After keeping him dangling for years, she wrote him that she had thought it over and had decided it would be best to remain good friends.

Above: Portrait of Mary Stuart by an anonymous artist. This painting hangs in the Uffizi Gallery in Florence. Above left: Lord Henry Darnley, the hapless second husband of the Queen of Scots. She married him on an impulse after Elizabeth put forth her own favorite, Lord Leicester. Elizabeth had let it be understood that if this union were to take place she would appoint her cousin heir to the English throne. Indeed, Mary's marriage to a Protestant would have rendered useless the intrigues of Spain and France, which were using her as a banner to rally Catholic interests. Mary soon lost all interest in Darnley and encouraged his assassination in 1567.

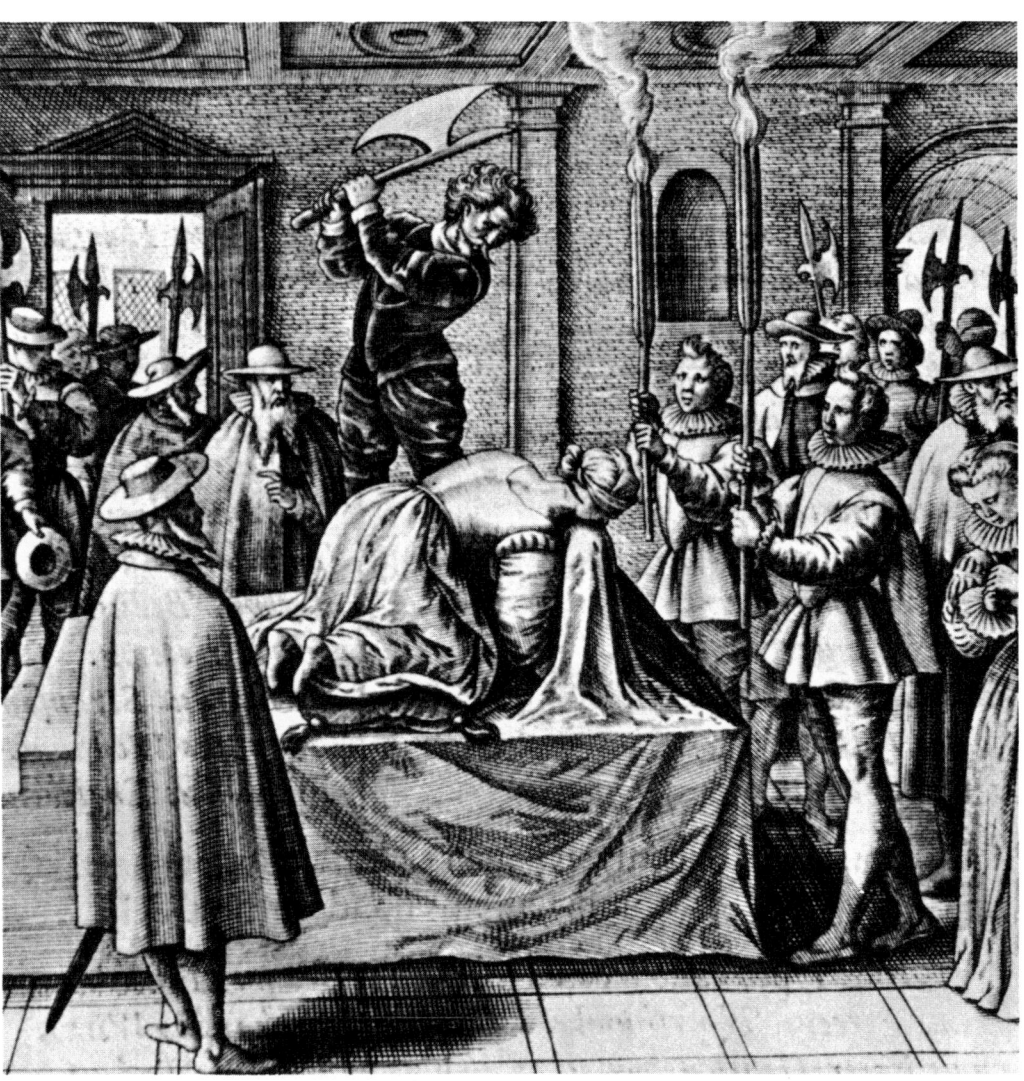

Heroine of so many plots perpetrated by others, Mary Stuart was finally undone by one of her own devising. She thought she was going to engineer a decisive coup, and her accomplices assured her of impending liberation. But Walsingham, Elizabeth's tireless Secretary of State, had been apprised of the plot by his highly efficient secret service. He decided that the moment had come to strike. Mary had signed a document consenting to the assassination of the Queen and to the invasion of the country. This was sufficient to bring her to trial and to convict her. Brought before the tribunal, Mary Stuart unwaveringly denied the evidence. Her constant refrain was that no one save God could pass judgment on princes; she owed no allegiance to English law because she had come to England asking for asylum, and she had been held prisoner against her will. Elizabeth signed the death warrant after much hesitation; then repented and assailed her ministers with recriminations and torrents of tears. But the messenger had already left for Fotheringay where, on February 8, 1587, Mary, Queen of Scots, placed her head on the block. She managed to cast an aura of martyrdom about her death. As one historian observed about the Stuarts, they did not know how to rule but they knew how to die.

Left: A painting of the last hours of Mary Stuart. Above: A 17th-century print showing her execution. The Queen of Scots carefully prepared the setting of her execution, knowing full well that she could make posterity forget a great many of her sins. She arrived on the ground floor of Fotheringay Castle where the block had been set up, after having kept everyone waiting for three hours. She was wearing black velvet and when her ladies-in-waiting removed her dress, she appeared in an underskirt made of blood-red silk, the color of martyrs. It took three blows of the axe to decapitate her. When the executioner tried to grasp her head to hold it up for inspection, it rolled away. Only a wig remained in his hand.

ENGLISH NAVAL STRATEGY

For years a "cold war" had been waged between Spain and England, with dangerous fires of attrition in Flanders—where Elizabeth backed the Protestants in their struggle against Philip II. And in Ireland—where his Catholic Majesty supported his fellow Catholics in their rebellion against the English. At one point, with no official break, the cold war broke out in open conflict. The year after Mary Stuart's death, Philip prepared a formidable fleet to attack the British coast. Even before the attack the Spaniards christened it the "Invincible Armada." The odds were in Philip's favor. However, in her 30 years' reign, Elizabeth had taught Europe to respect her strength. Long before, as a provision against a possible struggle, Elizabeth had ordered guns and cannons from the Low Countries. In July, 1588, the Armada appeared before Plymouth, 130 ships with over 3,000 guns and cannons, and 24,000 men led by the Duke of Medina-Sidonia. The plan of attack was that the enemy ships were to be boarded; then the Spanish infantry (the most formidable in Europe) would go into action. But Medina-Sidonia had not taken into account the type of small vessel used by his adversary. His heavy galleons with their myriad oars, suitable for the Mediterranean, were not easily manageable in English waters. The English, on the other hand, used small, agile sailing ships which had been outfitted with port and starboard cannons, which were introduced during the reign of Henry VIII. This arrangement had brought about a new strategy based on maneuverability and the range of artillery. When Drake and Hawkins, sailing in the open sea on July 21, 1588, opened fire on the slow and ponderous ships of the Armada, Medina-Sidonia, appalled, realized that his cannons were in no position to return the bombardment. The Spaniards retreated across the English Channel to the Isle of Wight. From the very beginning of the battle, the "Invincibles" had been beaten.

CATASTROPHIC DEFEAT OF THE ARMADA

The Spanish losses were not serious, however, and the Armada fell back on the Low Countries where the Duke of Parma was preparing an invasion force for England. Theoretically the invasion was still possible. But Parma was not ready, and while the huge fleet lingered at anchor before Calais, Elizabeth's sailors attacked it with fire ships laden with pitch and gunpowder. Forced to retreat again as panic spread among his crews, Medina-Sidonia sailed toward the North Sea, in the direction of the Irish coast. But this time even the elements were against him. The storm disrupted his retreat. Only one third of his ships returned home, together with about half of his men. The first "Battle of Britain" in modern history was won by Elizabeth's sailors and by the wind, and the decline of Spanish power had begun.

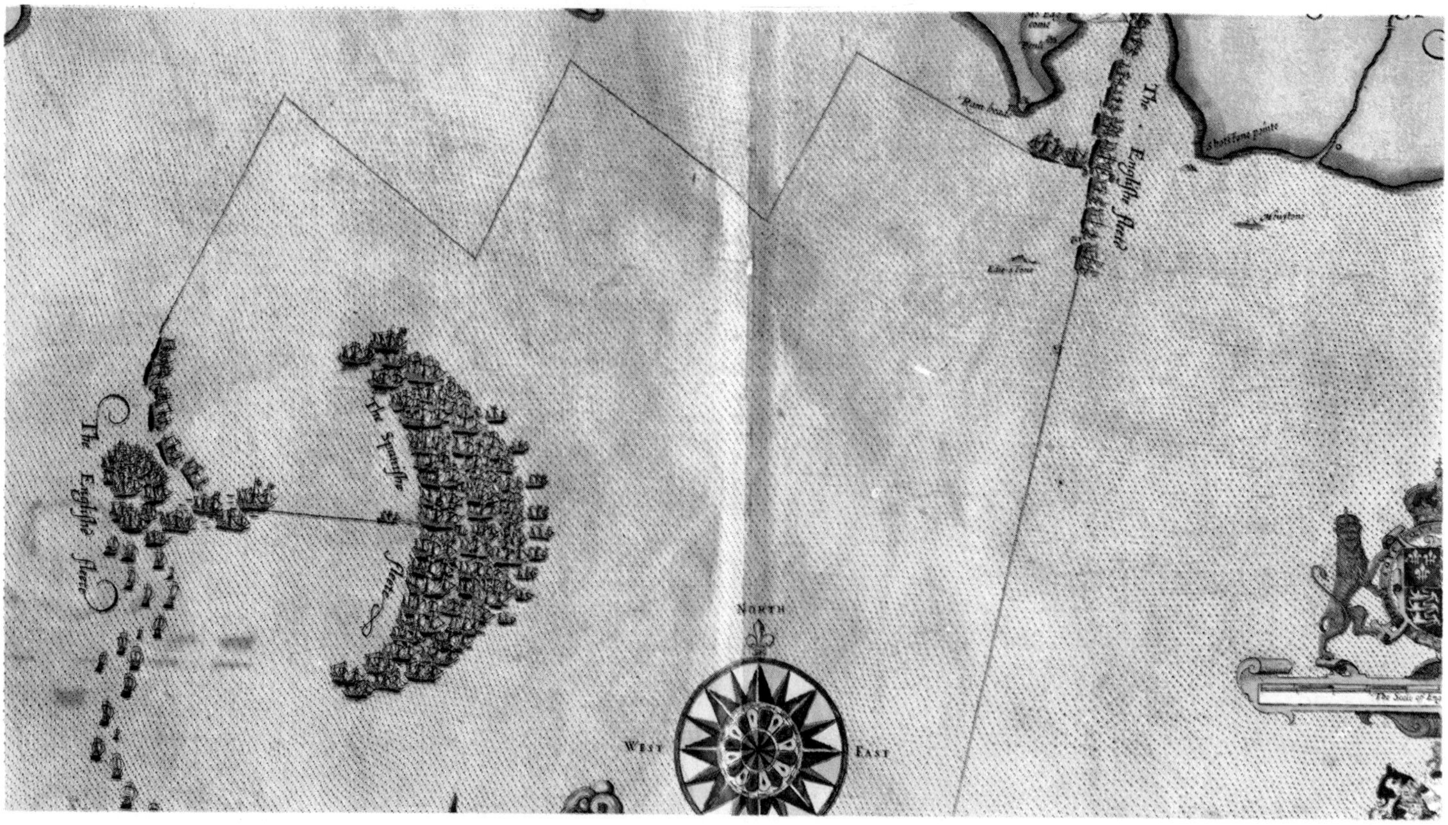

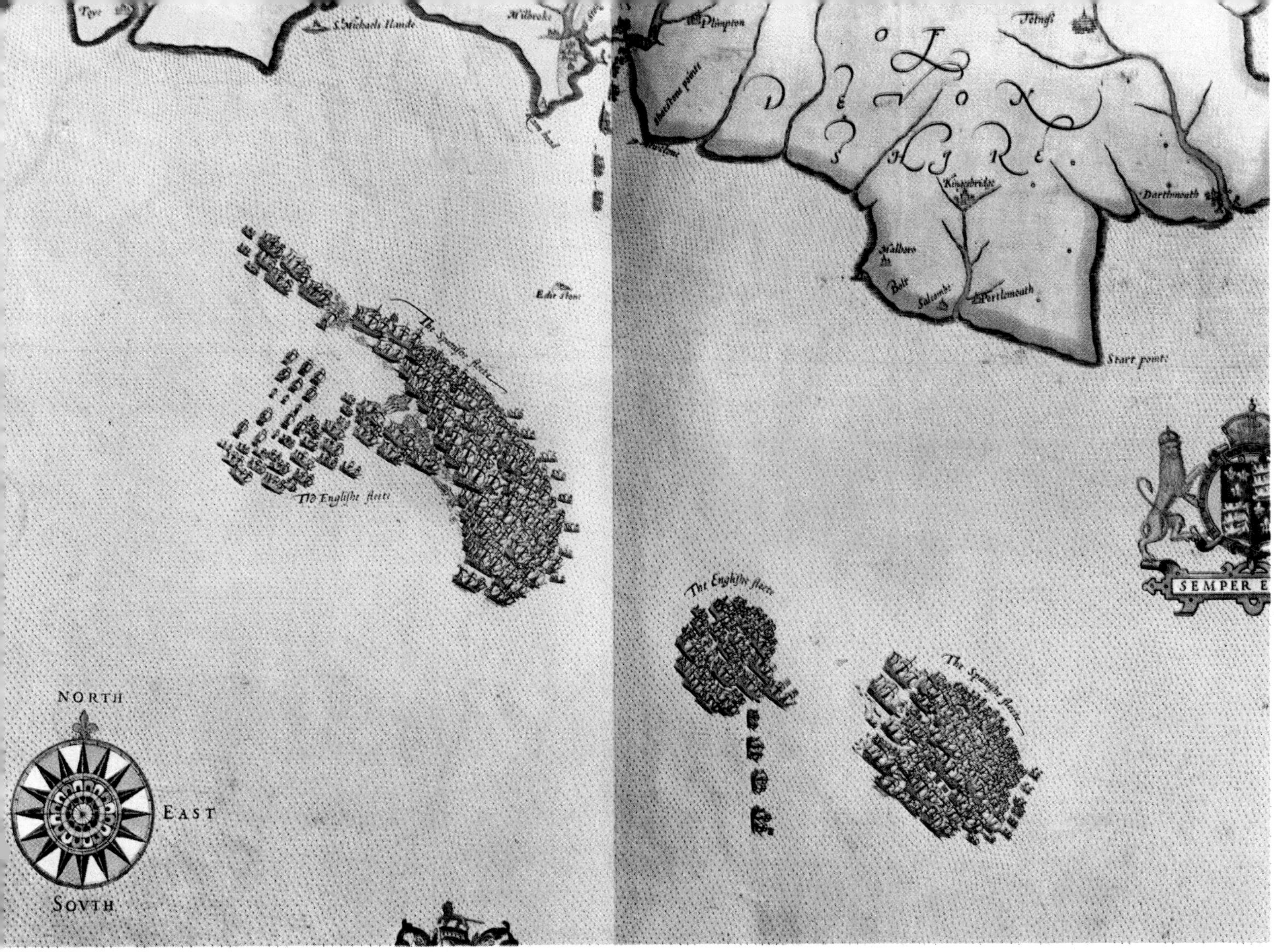

S. Michaels Ilande · Milbroke

Plimpton · Totnes

DEON SHIRE

Kingesbridge · Dartmouth

Malbaro · Salcombe · Portlemouth

Start point:

Eddi Ston:

The Spanish fleete

The English fleeti

The English fleete

The Spanish fleete

SEMPER E

NORTH

EAST

SOVTH

Ludworth · Corffe castel · Studlande pointe

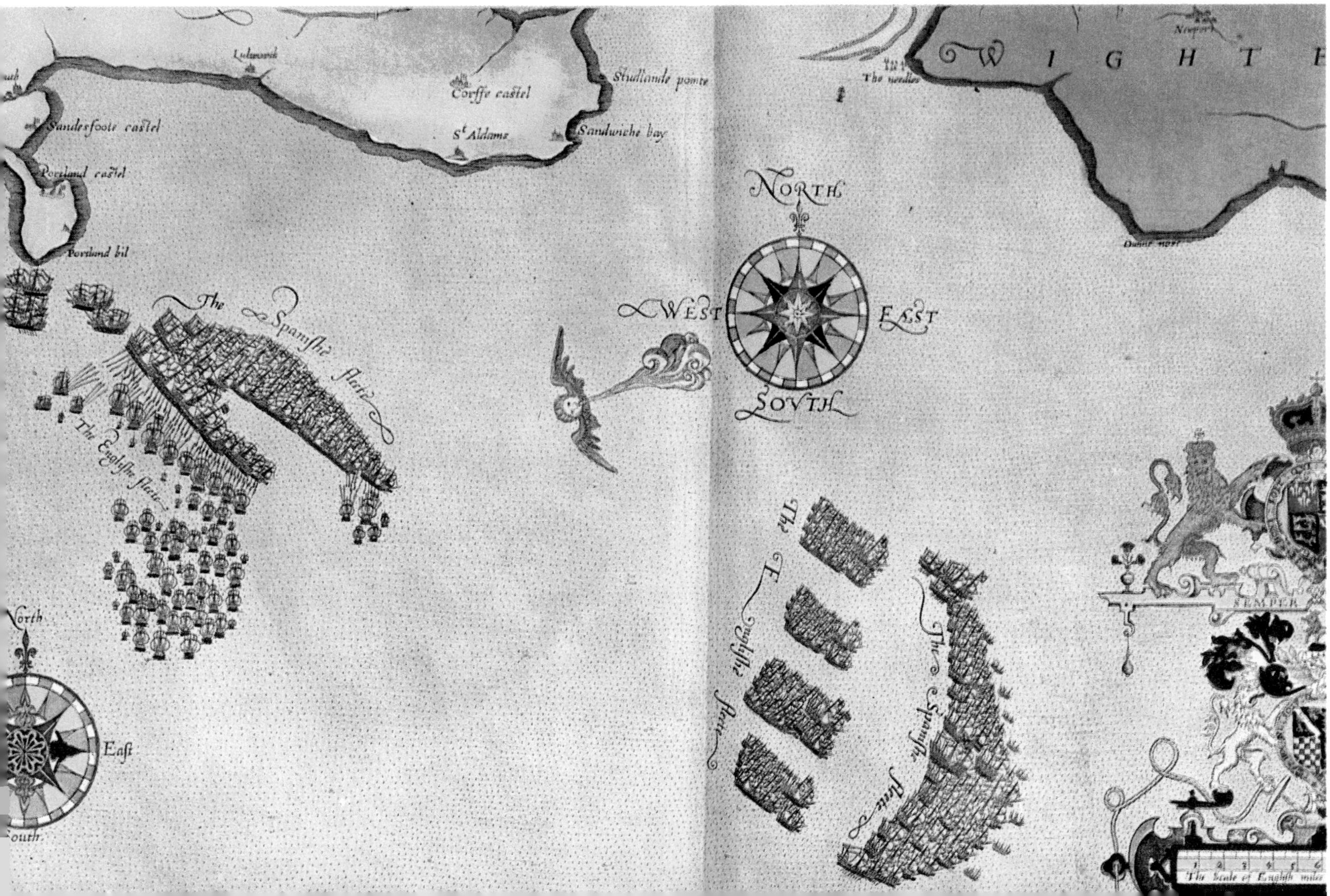

S.t Aldams · Sandwiche bay

WIGHT

Newport

The needles

Danet nosi

Sandersfoote castel

Portland castel

Portland hil

The Spanishe fleete

The Englishe fleete

North

East

South

NORTH

WEST · EAST

SOVTH

The Englishe fleete

The Spanish fleete

SEMPER

The Scale of English miles

Below: Queen Elizabeth in the famous "Armada Portrait." It was so named because in the background can be seen the ships that fought in the celebrated battle. The Sovereign herself went down among the troops, massed at Tilbury in expectation of an attack from enemy infantry, and made an impassioned speech. In Rome, at the tidings of the victory of the English ships over the "Invincible Armada," the English pupils of the Catholic Seminary, training for the spiritual reconquest of England, unexpectedly cheered the victory. For they were unwilling to have Catholicism restored to their country at the price of servitude to Spain. Philip II wrote to his Spanish bishops on October 13 about the battle. After having recapitulated the news they had already heard, he wrote that thanks should be rendered to the Lord that the losses suffered by the Armada had not been greater, given the weather and other adverse circumstances. He added that he attributed the partial salvage to their prayers.

1588:
AN INTOXICATING AND GLORIOUS SUMMER

Below: The setting for a ballet at the French court. Note the background and the illumination by candlelight. Even the Catholic powers were somewhat relieved by the news of the disaster of the Spanish Armada, for Spanish might had become worrisome, and not everyone was prepared to accept Philip as the champion of the True Faith. Sir Francis Drake, the most popular of the victors of the Armada, died on January 28, 1596, during an expedition to the West Indies, in which he had hoped to attack Panama and gain possession of Spanish gold. Afflicted with dysentery and fever, he died in the bay of Porto Bello murmuring, "We must have the gold." Hawkins also died during the same expedition.

The defeat of the Armada did not terminate the conflict. Like the "Battle of Britain" of our day, this one took place at the beginning, not the end, of the struggle. Actually, it dragged on for 14 more years, as many as remained to Elizabeth. And at the end there were neither victors nor vanquished. However, the importance of this battle fought in English waters did not escape the attention of Europe. Its meaning for the future was clear. For too long Philip had been dangerously confusing the interests of the Counter Reformation with those of Spain's imperialistic aims. The King received the news of the disaster while he was at prayer in the chapel of the Escurial, just where he had been 17 years earlier at the news of the victory over the Turks at the battle of Lepanto. Impassive now as he had been then, he continued his devotions. In England bonfires were lit on every hill. Elizabeth's popularity reached its zenith in the days that followed the great victory. The summer of 1588, the 30th of her reign, was England's most glorious and intoxicating period in the 16th century. Poets sang Elizabeth's praises under the name of "Gloriana", and she was transformed from a woman into a divinity. She even looked the part. In the portraits of her in her maturity her face is expressionless, rigid; her person is covered with gems, like some exotic goddess. There is a lunar reflection in the cold light that surrounds her, in the unnatural whiteness of her skin, reminiscent of the goddess of the night, the Virgin Diana. The people loved this idol. From a distance the wrinkles on her face could not be seen, her wigs could be taken for real hair, although their color was not quite natural. Even her missing teeth did not show, and her vitality was always the same: the Queen rode, the Queen hunted, she played on the virginal, danced complicated steps. But this woman masquerading as a goddess saw the shadows deepening around her. One by one the companions of her youth, of her work and struggles, of her amusements, her loves, died. Walsingham, stricken with gallstones, died in 1590, followed by Hatton, Heneage, Drake and Burghley. But the first to go, and her greatest personal loss, less than a month after the victory of the Armada, was her childhood playmate and favorite, Leicester. He was survived by his wife and a stepson, the Earl of Essex.

SHAKESPEARE

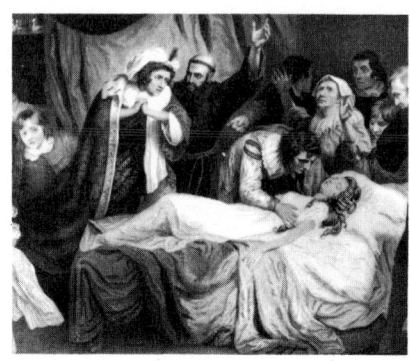 

The last 15 years of Elizabeth's reign saw the height of that literary and artistic flowering to which the Renaissance had given impetus in the first decades of the century. It was a veritable explosion of talent in which the theater played a preponderant part. In the latter part of the 1580's, when William Shakespeare, the son of a well-to-do country merchant, decided on a theatrical career, there were four fixed theaters in London. All of them were on the outskirts of the city, outside municipal jurisdiction, because of the many Puritans among the city councillors who considered plays to be an incentive to vice and disorderliness. Furthermore each company chose a protector at court whose name was used by the troupe. There were the men of the Earl of Warwick, those of Worcester and the "Admirals."

Above: Two scenes from "Romeo and Juliet" and "Hamlet" as seen through the eyes of 19th-century artists. Below: The Globe Theater shown in a 1647 print. Shakespeare not only acted here but also became part owner of the theater. It was later destroyed by fire. The theaters of the period copied the courtyards of inns where for a time actors performed their plays. The balconies on which the rooms opened were the forerunners of theater boxes for the "quality," while on foot the common people crowded in the courtyard and paid a penny admission. Opposite page,

top: Three 19th-century illustrations of "Richard III," the "Tempest" and the "Taming of the Shrew." Below, right: Probably portraits of Shakespeare (right) playing chess with Ben Jonson. The great English playwright and actor often performed for Queen Elizabeth. The theatrical season at court opened on the feast of St. Stephen and continued through the Christmas season. "Twelfth Night" was written by Shakespeare to be performed in the presence of the Queen on the eve of Epiphany, probably in the year 1599.

SHAKESPEAREAN ACTORS

The first time that Shakespeare's name appeared on a program was as an actor in a troupe called the Lord Chamberlain's Men. The patron was Lord Henry Hunsdon, Queen Elizabeth's cousin and court chamberlain. Later, Shakespeare and his company came under the direct patronage of King James I, a devotee of the stage. They were called the King's Men, which greatly enhanced their prestige. The term "Men" was an exact one, for the troupe consisted exclusively of males. The profession was considered suitable for men only and indeed required uncommon strength and dexterity. The demands of the scripts were such that the actor had to be acrobat, swordsman and dancer. The public was also demanding. The stage setting was only symbolic; it was the action that mattered. Duels had to be real duels (critics abounded on the floor as well as in the boxes). Flights, leaps, ladder ascents, all had to look authentic. In the scenes of violence, which were frequent, real blood had to flow. In order to achieve this, the actors wore a bladder filled with the blood of a lamb or of a kid under their clothes, which gushed forth to the delighted horror of the public. The large number of characters also required that each member of the cast take on four or five parts for each performance. Juliet, Ophelia, Portia, those fragile creations of Shakespeare's genius, were played by robust boys who were already shaving and whose voices had changed. Theatrical works in general were acquired from their authors, a picturesque and ill-fated breed of hapless poets, for very small sums of money. The author's rights were sold to a company for a sum that rarely exceeded £10 or £12. From then on, the script became the property of the actors. The latter seldom had it printed for fear that a rival company might appropriate it and add it to its own repertory. In this way a huge number of Elizabethan dramas were lost. Only when there was an outbreak of the plague or when the theaters were closed were plays published.

Below: Two London theaters at the end of the 16th century: the "Fortune" and the "Swan." The names also were reminiscent of the traditional names of the inns from which they stemmed. The banner flying from the roof indicated to the public that the theater was open. The "Swan" was built in 1595; the "Fortune" in 1599. The most active competitor of the "Chamberlain's Company," the one to which Shakespeare belonged, was the Admiral's (named for Lord Howard of Effingham, the commander of the English fleet against the Armada). Its most famous actor was Edward Alleyn. In Shakespeare's company, John Hemminge and Henry Condell were featured players. They later edited his plays.

ESSEX

Opposite page: Robert Devereux, Earl of Essex, from an oil painting by an unknown artist at the National Portrait Gallery in London. He was sentenced to a traitor's death (impaling and quartering), but the Queen changed the sentence to a simple beheading, which took place on February 21, 1601, in the courtyard of the Tower of London. He was 34 years old.

Directly below: A 19th-century print showing the Earl of Essex after he had burst into the Queen's bedchamber, at Nonesuch Castle, to beg her forgiveness for his mistakes in Ireland. Bottom of the page: Two contemporary prints of war scenes. Left: A satirical one of the Catholic League in France. Right: The Governor-General of Ireland, Sir Henry Sidney, departing from Dublin.

The latter part of Elizabeth's life was dominated by the figure of the Earl of Essex, Leicester's stepson. He had succeeded to his stepfather's duties as Master of the Horse and it was said that the young man, who was little more than 20 years old, of negligible intellect and coarse good looks, also replaced him in the Queen's heart. The gossip, avidly collected, was not, however, substantiated by any fact except the expressions of lowly flattery contained in his letters to her, a woman of 65, in which he swore he preferred her "beauty above all things." But false though this language might sound, it was certainly not peculiar to Essex. Indeed, it was common to all the court in its relations with the Sovereign. After all, the age of exaggeration, the baroque, had already begun. For her part, her attitude was rather that of an elderly aunt or a too-indulgent mother rather than that of a mistress. Certain liberties, which she had never allowed another living soul, and also certain rebuffs (like the famous slaps after the bickering on the question of Ireland) do not conjure up a bedroom atmosphere. Probably in the solitude of her declining years, Elizabeth saw in Essex the son she had never had. However, it would have been well had she heeded the judgment which Francis Bacon, who called himself Essex's friend, passed on him. "Madam, if you had my Lord of Essex here with a white staff in his hand, as my Lord of Leicester had, and continued him still about you for society to yourself, and for an honor and ornament to your attendance and Court in the eyes of your people, and in the eyes of foreign ambassadors, then were he in his right element. For to discontent him as you do, and yet put arms and power into his hands, may be a kind of temptation to make him prove cumbersome and unruly."

The prophecy was soon fulfilled. Essex considered himself a political and military genius; but his actions—cruising with Drake, or in France where he had gone to help Henry IV, or in Ireland where he hunted down rebels—were only a succession of blunders and losses. Every so often there were spurts of foolish bravura as pointless as they were costly. Even his last desperate attempt to make the people of London rebel and march against the Queen bears the same stamp of juvenile romanticism. Essex made the mistake that Mary Stuart had made: He failed to gauge correctly Elizabeth's character. He thought he could take advantage of the Queen because she was old, tired and maternal. Raleigh reported that he had said of her "that her mind had become as crooked as her carcass." He realized his mistake too late; a mistake which he paid for with his head.

SWEET ENGLAND'S PRIDE IS GONE

The last years of Elizabeth's life were shrouded in sadness and darkened by her mourning for Essex. Others wept for him too. "Sweet England's pride is gone" were the words of a popular ballad. To the masses of common people he had appeared like a fairy-tale knight despite his blunders and extravagances. Elizabeth's ladies-in-waiting often came upon her in some remote corner of the palace, her face bathed in silent tears. Everything around her was changing. The new times were difficult for her to adapt to, and she could no longer keep up with them. Her talents as economist and steward were not equal to dealing with the inflation; the help given the rebels in Flanders and the Huguenots in France ate up all the reserves so laboriously accumulated. Ireland, where the Spaniards continually threatened to build a base for invasion, was a bottomless pit into which were thrown endless sums of money and troops. During her last years, to meet mounting expenses, the Queen sold crown lands and jewels. But it was not enough. She was forced to ask Parliament for a new subsidy. In exchange, she promised to correct some of the tax abuses from which the House of Lords profited at the expense of the House of Commons. Her leavetaking from this Parliament in her famous "Golden Speech" summed up her life: "... Though God has raised me high, yet this I account the glory of my Crown, that I have reigned with your loves ... It is not my desire to live or reign longer than my life and reign shall be for your good. And though you have had, and may have, many mightier and wiser princes ... yet you never had, nor shall have, any that will love you better."

Opposite page, left: Elizabeth in her later years. Despite various ailments the Queen still had, until her last months, great energy. The first signs of her failing were gaps in her memory. Nonetheless she continued to ride, to dance and to give audiences standing up—the ambassadors often left her presence in a state of exhaustion. Below, left: 19th-century picture showing Elizabeth's last moments. She refused all medicine and seemed to put up no resistance to her sickness. Her cousin, Robert Carey, said that "She grew worse because she would be so." Her last days were tormented by insomnia, fever, restlessness and hallucinations. She died on March 24, 1603, at 3 A.M. Below: The conference at Somerset House for the peace negotiations between Spain and England in 1604, one year after Elizabeth's death. While the Queen was still alive, the English had forced the capitulation of the Spanish troops in Ireland. In the painting by Juan Pantoja de la Cruz the Spanish delegates are at the left; the English on the right. (Robert Cecil is in the right foreground.)

The Chariott drawne by foure Horses vpon which Charret stood the Coffin couered with purple Veluett and vpon that the reprefentation, The Canapy borne by six Knights.

THE SUCCESSION

Although her ministers had repeatedly begged her to appoint her successor, Elizabeth had always refused to do so. She remembered only too well her sister's last days when Mary lay dying in a semi-deserted palace, abandoned by the Court who had rushed to Hatfield to pay homage to her heir. She wanted no repetition of these scenes. However, some of the ministers, and Robert Cecil in particular—he had succeeded his father, William, Lord Burghley, as Secretary of State—had corresponded with the King of Scotland, James VI, to prepare for his accession to the throne. It fell to the lot of the pallid son of Mary Stuart and of her second husband, the ill-fated Darnley—or of the Italian Rizzio if the gossip was true—to become heir to the most splendid of the reigning houses of England and to unite the two kingdoms on either side of the Clyde. He was 37, a scholar and a stutterer. He wrote theological treatises and had two passions: hunting and the theater. From his royal castle in Edinburgh, James had kept in touch with the English court. Elizabeth could not last much longer. She had entered her 70th year, an age which few people in the 16th century ever reached. She had been on the throne for 44 years. Her coronation ring had become so tight that it had stopped the circulation and had to be sawed off. The symbolic meaning of this had filled her with sadness. The astrologer John Dee, at the beginning of 1603, had told her to beware of Whitehall, the royal palace in London. Accordingly, the court moved to Richmond House on the Thames, the seat of the house of Tudor, warmest of the royal residences. But the fires lit in the vast stone chimneys could not warm the cold that chilled her veins. From the end of February on she declined rapidly. She lay motionless against her cushions, sighing and refusing all food; she didn't want to go to bed because frightening visions assailed her. Once she saw herself in a dream, her body wasted, surrounded by flames. The day before her death she was so weak that she was carried to bed without objecting. To her advisers who consulted her on her successor, proposing the King of Scotland, she nodded her assent. Then, comforted by the prayers which the archbishop of Westminster intoned, she fell into a stupor from which she never emerged.

The image shows a contemporary print of the funeral procession with labels *footemen*, *Gentlemen Pentioners*, and a portrait of James Stuart.

Above: A contemporary print of the Queen's funeral procession. Upon the chariot was the "Representation," a wax effigy of the dead Queen clothed in royal robes and wearing the Crown. These funeral rites had been established in medieval times. The grief of the people was genuine and unprecedented in its intensity. A Catholic priest who was a prisoner in the Tower of London when the Queen was dying said the silence in the city was frightening. Left: James Stuart, the sixth of Scotland, the first of England, from a painting attributed to Jan de Critz. At the death of Elizabeth, couriers who had been held in readiness by

Cecil brought the news to Edinburgh. The King of Scotland and Lord Burghley's son had been writing letters to each other for some time. Once they were almost caught when Elizabeth, seeing the messenger arriving with the mail from Scotland, ordered the satchel to be brought to her. Cecil, knowing the compromising nature of its contents, did not panic. Remembering the Queen's aversion to bad odors, he said that before giving her the satchel he would have it purified of the "stink" of the rough Scottish Highlanders. The Queen agreed. He removed the incriminating evidence before turning over its contents to her.

IN THE GLORY OF WESTMINSTER ABBEY

Elizabeth has been resting for over three and a half centuries in the glory of Westminster Abbey. This abbey, officially known as the Collegiate Church of St. Peter, founded by Edward the Confessor, was the first example of Norman style in England. Here all but two British monarchs have been crowned: Edward V, who died in the Tower, and Edward VIII, who abdicated before his coronation. It was also here that Henry VII, Elizabeth's grandfather and founder of the Tudor dynasty, caused the splendid chapel which bears his name to be built on the site of the Lady Chapel. All of his descendants rest near him. Elizabeth's tomb, with its ornate marble canopy, shows the baroque influence in its elaborate decoration. A reclining marble effigy of the Queen lies on top of the sarcophagus. Sculptured according to the realistic tradition of the era, the effigy bears all the attributes of power. Her head, crowned with a diadem and reposing on an embroidered pillow, rests lightly in the sleep of eternity.

No period in English history is as rich in splendor and adventure as the Elizabethan era. Elizabeth came to the throne of a country just emerging from the Middle Ages, impoverished and torn by religious dissention. When she died, she left it in a state of prosperity, international prestige, and an unsurpassed flowering of the arts. It was truly then that England became in the eyes of all the world "Merrie England." The greatest praise bestowed upon her came from a man whom circumstances forced to oppose her, Sixtus V. "She certainly is a great queen, and were she only a Catholic she would be our dearly beloved daughter. Just see how she governs! She is only a woman, only mistress of half an island, and yet she makes herself feared by Spain, by France, by the Empire, by all." This admirable Queen was also an "enchanted spirit" in the words of another of her adversaries. Born in an era when women were beginning to emerge from the home to take their part in the world, Elizabeth knew how to use her femininity, but she never allowed it to cloud her judgment. During the duel that lasted almost 30 years with Mary Stuart, victory went to the wiser queen who knew how to govern her passions and keep her head. The two enemies, at rest now, sleep near each other in the glory of Westminster.

1533—September 7: Born in Greenwich to Henry VIII and Anne Boleyn, his second wife.
1534—Beginning of the Anglican schism.
1536—Anne Boleyn beheaded. Ten days later Henry VIII marries Jane Seymour.
1537—Birth of Edward VI. Twelve days later death of his mother, Jane Seymour.
1544—Act of Parliament establishing Mary (her older half sister) and Elizabeth in the succession. Henry had previously declared them illegitimate.
1547—Death of Henry VIII; Edward VI succeeds him.
1553—Death of Edward VI. Succeeded by his half-sister Mary, later known as "Bloody Mary." Elizabeth locked up for several months in the Tower. Mary marries Philip, heir to the Spanish throne and son of the Emperor Charles V.
1556—At his father's abdication, Mary's husband becomes Philip II of Spain and leaves his wife in England.
1558—January 8: England loses Calais, her last foothold on the European continent. November 17: death of Mary Tudor after she had named Elizabeth as her successor.
1559—January: Coronation of Elizabeth I. April 2: Peace of Cateau-Cambresis. Acts of Supremacy and of Uniformity (imposition of the Book of Common Prayer). July: Revolt in Scotland of the Calvinist, John Knox.
1560—Elizabeth opens hostilities against Scotland. Treaty of Edinburgh. Death of Francis II, husband of Mary Stuart, Queen of Scotland, and Elizabeth's cousin.
1561—Birth of Francis Bacon.
1562—Elizabeth is stricken with smallpox, but she recovers.

1564—April 23: Birth of William Shakespeare.
1564-67—Buccaneer activities of Hawkins (secretly aided and abetted by the Crown) in the Caribbean Sea.
1565—Mary Stuart married to Henry Darnley.
1566—June 19: Mary Stuart gives birth to the future King James VI of Scotland (James I of England).
1567—May 15: death of Mary Stuart's second husband. She marries the Earl of Bothwell. Rebellion breaks out and Mary is forced to abdicate.
1568—Mary Stuart takes refuge in England.
1569-70—Catholic uprisings led by Lord Northumberland and Lord Dacre put down.
1570—Pius V excommunicates Elizabeth.
1572—April: Treaty of Blois with France. June 2: Duke of Norfolk condemned to death. August 24: Massacre of St. Bartholomew's Day in France.
1573—Diplomatic victory of Elizabeth: ports in the Low Countries reopened to English goods.
1577—Departure of Drake for the Pacific.
1580—Philip II annexes Portugal and all her overseas possessions.
1584—Eviction of the Spanish Ambassador from England.
1585—Spain confiscates English merchant ships in the Port of Bilbao. Agreement with the Low Countries. New expedition led by Drake.
1586—A new plot against Elizabeth, hatched by Babington with the connivance of Mary Stuart, is uncovered.
1587—February 8: After 18 years of imprisonment Mary, Queen of Scots, is condemned to

death. April 17: Drake with a naval squadron attacks Cadiz.
1588—July 21: defeat of the "Invincible" Spanish Armada.
1589—April: new English expedition against Spanish ships at Lisbon.
1593—Henry IV of France leaves the Protestant Church and is converted to Catholicism.
1596—Death of Drake and Hawkins in the Caribbean during the course of a new expedition. A fleet of 80 English ships opposite Cadiz. Philip II of Spain launches a new "Armada" against England, which is dispersed by a hurricane.
1597—Expedition of the English fleet, commanded by Essex, against the port of Ferrol. Spain sends a third Armada against England. This one also dispersed by unfavorable weather.
1598—Death of Elizabeth's counselor, William Cecil. His son Robert succeeds him. May 2: Henry IV of France concludes a separate peace with Philip II (in violation of the understanding between him and Elizabeth). Death of Philip II. Defeat of the English in Ireland by rebels led by the Earl of Tyrone.
1599—Essex, the Queen's favorite, sent to Ireland.
1601—Execution of Essex, convicted of conspiring against Elizabeth. Tenth and last meeting of Parliament during Elizabeth's reign: abolition of privileged monopolies granted to private citizens.
1602—Defeat of the Irish insurgents.
1603—March 24: death of Elizabeth at the age of 70 after 44 years of reign. With her ends the Tudor Dynasty. James VI of Scotland comes to the throne as James I of England, thereby uniting the two kingdoms.

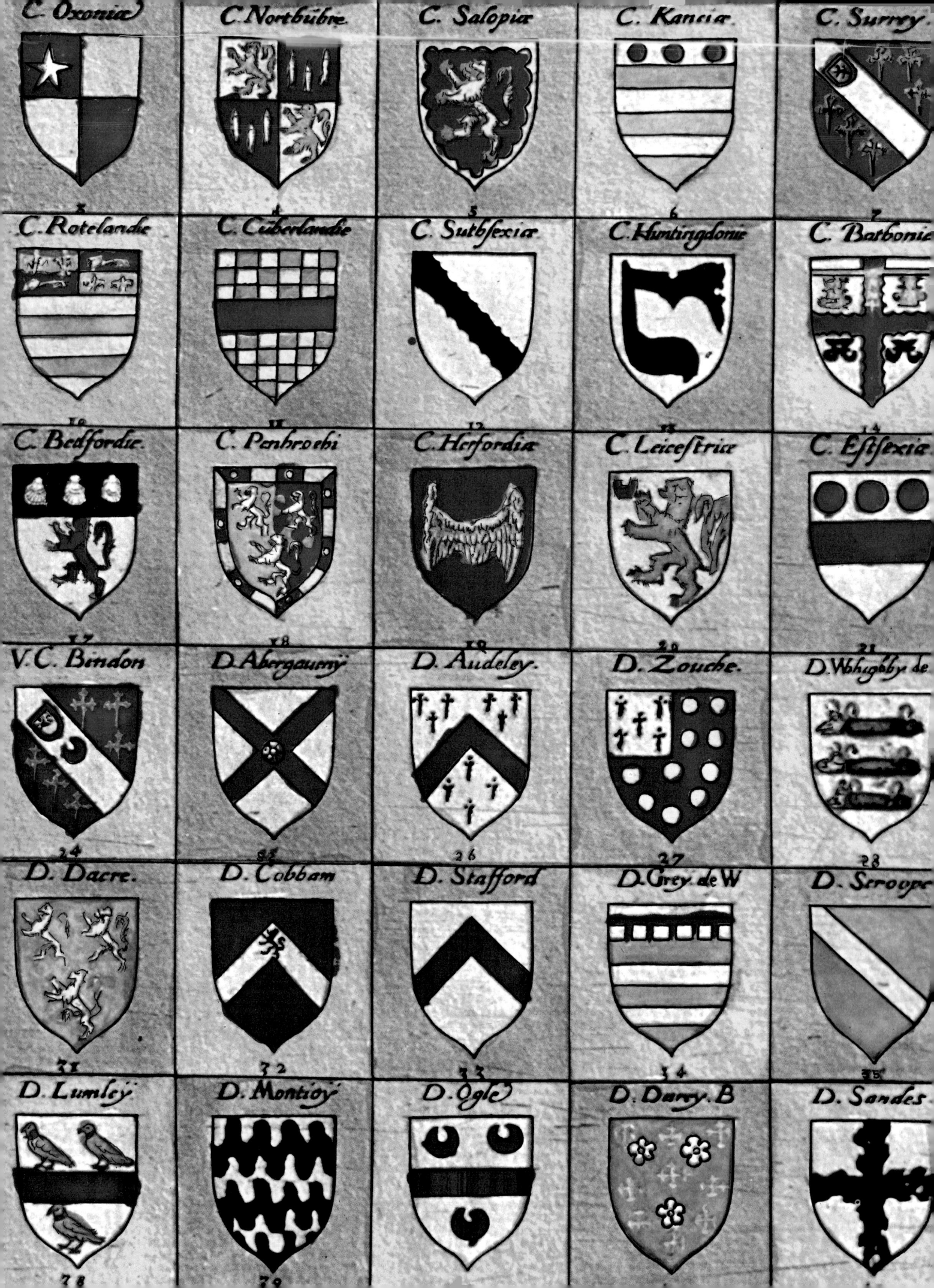

C. Oxonia	C. Nortbūbrie	C. Salopiæ	C. Kancia	C. Surrey
3	4	5	6	7
C. Rotelandie	C. Cūberlandie	C. Suthfexiæ	C. Huntingdonie	C. Barbonie
10	11	12	13	14
C. Bedfordie.	C. Penbrochi	C. Herfordia	C. Leicestriæ	C. Eſſexiæ
17	18	19	20	21
V. C. Bindon	D. Abergauuny	D. Audeley.	D. Zouche	D. Wbhugobye de
24	25	26	27	28
D. Dacre.	D. Cobbam	D. Stafford	D. Grey de W	D. Scroope
31	32	33	34	35
D. Lumley	D. Montioy	D. Ogle	D. Darcy. B	D. Sandes
78	79			